1001 Awesome ANIMAL FACTS

It's a jungle out there!

Marc Powell

ARCTURUS

FIFE COUNCIL	
914053	
PETERS	14-Sep-2009
J590	£6.99
JAN	BAND

This edition published in 2009 by Arcturus Publishing Limited
26/27 Bickels Yard, 151–153 Bermondsey Street,
London SE1 3HA

ISBN: 978-1-84837-229-0
CH000493EN

Author: Mark Powell
Editor: Fiona Tulloch

Cover goblin illustration by Steve Beaumont

Design and illustration by Dynamo Ltd

Printed in Singapore

CONTENTS

1001 Awesome ANIMAL FACTS

The world is a wonderful place filled with all manner of amazing creatures. Everything that crawls, flies, slithers, swings or swims has its own story to tell.

From the dawn of the dinosaurs right up to the present day, creatures all around the world have been doing amazing things that are just normal to them. For example, did you know that the grebe bird eats feathers and feeds them to their young even though they can't digest them? Or that beavers are sometimes parachuted into remote river areas to build dams and prevent flooding? Don't think you have to travel the world, or even through time, to be impressed — even your supposedly 'everyday' pets will become loads more interesting after you've read about their weird and wacky habits.

It may get a bit gross in places. In fact, it's definitely going to get a little bit icky and may put you off your dinner. You'll discover the disgusting habits of the animals that you thought were oh-so cute and the incredible ways of those that you may have thought were a bit boring.

Awesome Ape and Monkey Facts

(Free extras, not part of your 1001 facts!)

Most animals try to blend in with their surroundings but the mandrill has decided it's better to look good than to be able to hide easily. With its red nose, blue cheeks and orange beard it's not easy to miss. Add to that a big blue behind and you have one truly multicoloured monkey.

The pygmy marmoset is the world's smallest primate – it's the size of a hamster!

They say a chimpanzee can learn to recognize itself in a mirror but no other monkey or ape can. (Maybe they're just not as vain as chimpanzees.)

Proboscis monkeys have huge, funny noses. They are so big that they can measure a quarter of their total body length. That's like you having a nose as long as your arm!

Finally, a quick tip for you: next time you see a gorilla with the sniffles, it's probably not a good idea to offer him a tissue, as gorillas can catch colds and many other illnesses through contact with humans. In fact, going anywhere near a gorilla is probably not a good idea at the best of times…

Look but don't touch!

Watch your pets with an observant eye, get out your magnifying glass in the garden, even try hypnotizing a chicken if you know a friendly one nearby. But please, please be kind to animals. Remember, they are living things and will defend themselves and their environments if they feel threatened, which could lead to some nasty injuries. Pay closer attention to nature but make sure all you do is observe. A bit like teachers and parents, no matter how gross, stinky or nasty they seem, they have feelings too…

Prehistoric Predator
Facts

1001 Awesome Animal Facts

The word dinosaur means 'terrible lizard'.

In 1676, a huge *femur* (thigh bone) was found in England by Reverend Robert Plot. It was thought at the time that the bone belonged to a giant!

In 1780, the remains of Mosasaurus were seized by the French army and were taken from the Netherlands all the way to Paris!

Spinosaurus was the largest meat-eating dinosaur. Even though it looked big and scary, its favourite food was fish!

Cells discovered in a T. rex bone have DNA that so closely resembles that of a bird, that some scientists believe T. rex would have tasted like chicken!

Around 50,000 years ago, ancient Australia was home to Procoptodon, the world's largest kangaroo. It was twice the size of today's kangaroos.

Some dinosaurs, such as Parasaurolophus, used their large noses to control their body temperature by adjusting the amount of air they breathed in.

Four in every five dinosaur discoveries are made by amateurs rather than by scientists.

It was possible to tell the age of a *Mastodon* (ancient relative of modern elephants) by cutting into the fat around its tusks. The rings in the fat could be counted to determine its age, just like a tree!

Approximately 440 different kinds of dinosaurs are currently known to have existed.

Unlike in the movies, Velociraptor did not kill its prey with its razor-sharp claw. It used its claws to hang on to its prey while attacking it with its teeth, a bit like lions do today.

Some *Pteranodons* (flying reptiles, like dinosaurs) used their pointy heads as an air-brake for landing – they would turn sideways to catch the wind and slow themselves down.

When dinosaurs first appeared during the Triassic period, (248–206 million years ago) the earth had just one huge continent called Pangea.

Horses evolved around 50 million years ago, soon after dinosaurs became extinct.

Over 100 million years ago, crocodiles were twice the size they are now.

The gigantic dinosaur Sauroposeidon could stretch its neck out 17 metres/55 feet. That's the same height as four double-decker buses stacked on top of each other!

Over 390 million years ago, prehistoric swamps were home to sea scorpions larger than humans. Discovered in Germany, one fossilized beast was a whopping 2.5 metres/ 8 feet long!

Scientists use dentists' drills to clean dinosaur bones.

Quetzalcoatlus was the biggest flying creature ever. It had enormous wings and was the size of a modern two-seater aeroplane!

Fossilized cockroaches have been found to be 300 million years old. This means they existed 100 million years before the dinosaurs!

On the tiny Arctic island of Spitsbergen, just off the coast of Norway, researchers discovered a fossil graveyard holding a total of 28 plesiosaurs and ichthyosaurs. Why they all died in that particular area is a mystery.

Because the pigment (colour) is not preserved in fossils, nobody knows what colour the dinosaurs were. Many palaeontologists think they were earthy colours like grey, green or brown.

T. rex ate the equivalent in meat of 290 adult humans every year.

The first dinosaur, Eoraptor, appeared around 225 or 230 million years ago and was about the size of a dog.

Scientists believe that dinosaurs talked to each other. From examining their head shapes, it's thought that T. rex probably had a deep raspy call, a Hadrosaur sounded like a honking goose and Apatosaurus sounded like a herd of snorting horses!

T. rex could run no faster than 32 kilometres/20 miles per hour. If it fell over while running, it probably would have died as its arms were too short to break its fall.

A massive sloth called Megatherium roamed the earth as recently as 8,000 years ago. If the huge elephant-sized beast hadn't been wiped out by human hunting they'd still be alive today!

The woolly mammoth, which roamed the earth around 10,000 years ago, had tusks that stretched a massive 4.8 metres/16 feet. That's nearly three times the length of an elephant's tusks.

There is a Harry Potter dinosaur! Children viewing a newly discovered Pachycephalosaurus skull in Indianapolis, USA, suggested naming the dinosaur *Dracorex hogwartsia* – Dracorex meaning 'dragon king' and 'hogwartsia' after the famous young wizard's school.

Palaeontologists know what the dinosaurs ate because they study fossilized *coprolite* – that's right, giant dino poop!

Dakosaurus was a water creature with a head like a meat-eating dinosaur but the flippers and tail of a fish. What a combination!

Mosquitoes have been buzzing around the planet, sucking blood for around 200 million years. Even dinosaurs could have been bitten by them!

The largest coprolite discovered measures 50 centimetres/19.5 inches wide and was produced by a T. rex in Saskatchewan, Canada, more than 65 million years ago.

The largest brain of any dinosaur in relation to its body size belonged to the Troodon. It's thought that it was cleverer than any reptile living today.

Earth was home to nearly twice as many plant-eating dinosaurs as meat-eating dinosaurs.

Ever wonder what happened to Brontosaurus? It was 'discovered' in 1879 but only later did scientists realize that it had already been discovered in 1877 and was already called Apatosaurus!

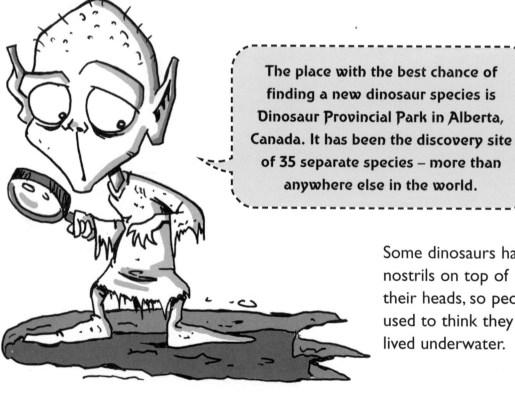

The place with the best chance of finding a new dinosaur species is Dinosaur Provincial Park in Alberta, Canada. It has been the discovery site of 35 separate species – more than anywhere else in the world.

Some dinosaurs had nostrils on top of their heads, so people used to think they lived underwater.

Fossil evidence suggests the huge shark Megalodon, which was around between 18 million and 2 million years ago, hunted large whales by biting off their tails and flippers.

The first dinosaur to appear in a novel was a Megalosaurus, mentioned in the first paragraph of Charles Dickens' *Bleak House* in 1852.

Brachiosaurus had high blood pressure – it was four times that of a human's, in fact. Why? Because it needed to pump blood all the way up its massive neck!

The first piece of dinosaur to make it into space was a fragment of Maisaura bone and eggshell which flew on a Spacelab II mission in 1985.

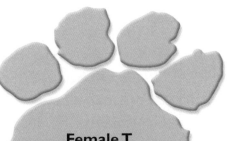

Female T. rexes are believed to have been bigger than males.

Leonardo, a 77-million-year-old Brachylophosaurus fossil discovered in Montana, USA, is unique for being the only fossil ever discovered completely covered in skin. The skin preserved its internal organs too, giving scientists an amazing insight into how dinosaurs' bodies worked.

Woolly mammoths had a flap of hairy skin that protected their bottoms from the cold!

Diplodocus may have been one of the biggest animals to ever exist, but its brain was only the size of a human fist!

Fish have been on Earth for more than 450 million years and were long-term residents of the planet long before dinosaurs arrived.

The most complete T. rex skeleton ever found has a name: Sue! It was named after Sue Hendrickson, the amateur palaeontologist who discovered the remains in 1990.

In 1853 a life-sized model of an Iguanodon was constructed for the opening of the Crystal Palace Exhibition in London. Sir Richard Owen and 20 other gentlemen dined inside the dinosaurs, feasting on mock turtle soup, pigeon pie and lots of wine. Very strange…

The oldest reference to dinosaur fossils is in a Chinese book written between AD265 and AD317. It describes the discovery of 'dragon bones' in the Sichuan Province of China.

T. rex's teeth were four times longer than a modern tiger's.

In 1924 some fossilized dinosaur remains were discovered on top of a nest of empty eggs. Scientists thought that the dinosaur had eaten the eggs, so named the dinosaur Oviraptor, meaning 'egg thief'.

Palaeontologists believe that Diplodocus could snap its tail like a whip, generating a sonic boom as loud as 200 decibels. When the Space Shuttle takes of from its launch pad it averages around 180 decibels – so that's pretty loud for a tail.

Struthiomimus, a funny emu-like creature, was the fastest running dinosaur and could easily outrun a modern racehorse.

Recent studies have suggested that the underwater predator Dunkleosteus had a more powerful bite than T. rex.

T. rex has an Asian cousin! Its name is *Tyrannosaurus bataar*.

Megalodon's name means 'big tooth' in Greek.

Velociraptor is often shown in movies as being bigger than it really was. It was actually only the size of a large dog...and had feathers, too!

Megarachne is the largest spider ever discovered. It roamed the earth around 290 million years ago and measured 50 centimetres/20 inches across. Not so incy wincy!

The plant eater Leaellynasaura is named after a little girl, Laellyn Rich, whose parents first discovered the dinosaur and named it after her!

At over 3 metres/10 feet long, Triceratops had one of the largest skulls of any land animal ever discovered.

Experts work out how fast dinosaurs moved by measuring the distance between footprints fossilized in mud.

Despite what you may have seen in the movies, a Stegosaurus never actually saw a T. rex. In fact, Stegosaurus died out around 80 million years before T. rex ever set foot on the planet!

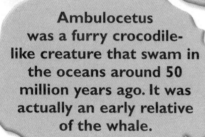

Ambulocetus was a furry crocodile-like creature that swam in the oceans around 50 million years ago. It was actually an early relative of the whale.

The most complete Stegosaurus skeleton ever discovered was found in the Rocky Mountains in Colorado, USA. It was so huge that it had to be airlifted by an army helicopter.

A giant guinea pig the size of a buffalo lived in South America eight million years ago. It must've needed one huge cage…

The world's oldest dinosaur fossils are 230 million years old and were discovered in Madagascar.

Maisaura and Leaellynasaura are the only two dinosaurs with female names.

In the *Jurassic Park* movies, the roar of the T. rex was a combination of tiger, alligator and baby elephant sounds!

Ankylosaurus was the most heavily armoured dinosaur, with thick plates and sharp spikes covering 90 per cent of its body – even its eyelids!

Andrewsarchus, a large wolf-like predator from around 45 million years ago, had a length from nose to tail of 3.5 metres/12 feet. It was the largest meat-eating mammal to ever roam the planet.

Eight-year old Christopher James Wolfe discovered Zuniceratops in 1996 in New Mexico, USA. Just shows that you're never too young to start dinosaur hunting!

Although many prehistoric creatures were bigger than today's animals, the blue whale remains the biggest ocean creature to have ever existed. Not surprising, considering its heart is the size of a small car!

Only 10 per cent of the animal species that have ever existed are still alive today.

A dinosaur discovered in Madagascar in 2001 was named *Masiakasaurus knopfleri* after Mark Knopfler, the lead singer of the rock group Dire Straits. Theirs was the palaeontologist's favourite music to dig to!

The closest living relative of the T. rex is the chicken. Incredible!

Some dinosaurs swallowed stones which helped to break up the food in their stomachs. Sounds weird? Birds still do it today!

The king of the prehistoric sharks, Megalodon, was two and a half times longer and 30 times heavier than today's great white shark.

The only way to kill an Ankylosaurus was to attack its soft underbelly.

Fragments of the dinosaur *Amphicoelias fragillimus*, discovered in 1877, suggest that it was the largest dinosaur ever. Scientists estimate that it would have been longer than a blue whale and had a weight equal to about 1,400 adult humans.

Archelon was a huge sea turtle that roamed the seas during the time of the dinosaurs. If you think modern day turtles are big, try this one – it was about the size of a family car!

A perfectly frozen baby mammoth was discovered in Siberia in 2007. The specimen was so well preserved that it still had some hair on it!

If the famous Loch Ness monster of Scotland actually exists, scientists claim that it could only weigh about 31 kilograms/67 pounds as there is only enough fish in the loch to feed a small meat eater. That would make Nessie around the size of a greyhound!

Oryctodromeus was like a prehistoric rabbit! The dinosaur built burrows under ground to raise its babies and hide from predators.

The last Ice Age (10,000 years ago) was a time of many massive versions of animals we know today including a 2.5-metre/8-foot beaver that roamed across modern day North America.

Scientists originally thought that *Sauropods* (long-necked dinosaurs that walked on four feet) had a second brain. The mystery bump in their spinal chord was actually the nerve centre that controlled the hind legs and tail. This was actually larger than their tiny brains!

Evidence of microscopic life forms discovered in Greenland indicates that there could have been life on earth as far back as 3,800 million years ago.

Giganotosaurus was a giant predator, but quite a stupid one. Its tiny brain was the size and shape of a banana!

Dinosaurs' upper teeth had a heavy coating of *enamel* (a hard glassy substance) on the outside, as did their inside lower teeth. This meant that as they bit their teeth together, they sharpened themselves. Clever.

The male Stethacanthus (an ancient shark) had a huge fin on top of its head in the shape of an ironing board!

The name *Megalograptus* means 'big writing' – when fossilized, its spindly legs looked like pencil markings on the rock!

Dimetrodon, the creature with a huge sail-fin on its back, was not actually a dinosaur. It died out almost 220 million years before the likes of T. rex even existed.

Megalodon sharks had mouths so large that they could have swallowed five adult humans in a single gulp.

The first animal to move from water to land was Megalograptus, a giant sea scorpion that lived 450 million years ago.

The tiny *Micropachycephalosaurus* has the longest name of any dinosaur.

Some ancient sea-dwelling lizards could detach their tails from their bodies so that they could give predators the slip!

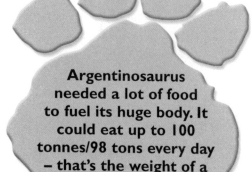

Argentinosaurus needed a lot of food to fuel its huge body. It could eat up to 100 tonnes/98 tons every day – that's the weight of a blue whale!

One of the fiercest marine predators ever was Dunkleosteus. It would eat anything – fossils have even been found with the half-digested remains of other Dunkleosteuses inside.

When Phil Manning of the University of Manchester discovered a set of Titanosaur tracks, he preserved the tracks by using lasers to build a 3D image of the site. Scientists studied this instead, leaving the tracks intact.

A T. rex wouldn't have heard you scream if it attacked you. Scientists in Germany have found that the hearing range of the larger dinosaurs was pretty terrible, with Brachiosaurus being almost completely deaf.

Stegosaurus had a brain the size of a walnut!

Feathered
Facts

The vampire finch is so called because of its habit of pecking other birds and feeding on their blood!

Turkeys have been known to have heart attacks. When the US Air Force began tests to break the sound barrier they found entire fields of turkeys on the flight paths dead from the shock of the sonic booms.

When humans colonized the island of Mauritius in 1600, the dodo – a bird native to the island – became extinct just 100 years later.

The *guanay cormorant* uses its own dried faeces to make its nest.

Some owls can turn their heads round at a 270-degree angle. They have to do this because their eyes are too large to move in their eye sockets.

The turkey vulture covers its legs in faeces to keep cool when it is hot.

Vultures sometimes eat so much that they become too heavy to fly. They have to vomit to bring their weight down again.

If you laid end to end all the earthworms eaten by a baby robin in one day, they would stretch to 4 metres/14 feet.

Pitohui birds eat a certain type of beetle that makes their skin and feathers poisonous to predators.

The nest of the *vervain hummingbird* is half the size of a walnut shell and its eggs are only 1 centimetre/0.4 inch long.

The emperor penguin regularly dives to depths of 534 metres/1,751 feet. The world record for the deepest human scuba dive is 308 metres/1,010 feet.

The *bar-tailed godwit* migrates further in a single trip than any other bird. Each year it travels non-stop from Alaska to New Zealand in just nine days and loses over half of its body weight on the trip.

Hoatzin chicks from South America can climb trees. They use special claws to move around until their wings are strong enough for them to fly.

The bird with the lowest number of feathers is the ruby-throated hummingbird. It only has 940 of them!

A bird's instinct to migrate is so strong that even birds in cages with artificial light and heat will try to fly along the same migrating pattern as wild birds.

The whistling swan has the most feathers of any bird, with over 25,000. The ruby-throated hummingbird must be jealous…

Penguins can jump nearly 2 metres/6 feet into the air... but they can't fly!

Geese have been found flying at heights of up to 8 kilometres/5 miles above the ground. A jumbo jet cruises at around 12 kilometres/7.5 miles!

Not all birds have been proven to have a sense of smell.

The feathers of a pigeon weigh more than its bones!

European starlings see everything in the ultraviolet range of light. This means that rather than seeing you as a normal person they actually see you as a figure of glowing light.

If you keep an albatross on a boat, it can get seasick.

A falcon can spot an object the size of a mouse from 1.5 kilometres/1 mile away.

Penguin urine accounts for nearly 3 per cent of the ice in Antarctic glaciers.

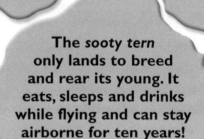

The *sooty tern* only lands to breed and rear its young. It eats, sleeps and drinks while flying and can stay airborne for ten years!

The *southern giant petrel* likes to vomit smelly stomach oils and regurgitated food at predators or nosy humans.

American turkey vultures help humans detect broken underground fuel pipes. The leaking fuel smells like carrion (the dead animals they eat). The clusters of birds standing around leaks show the engineers where repairs are needed.

The chicken is the most common bird on the planet, with over 24 billion of them worldwide.

Owls swallow their prey (mostly mice and voles) whole. The parts they cannot digest, like fur and bones, are formed into small pellets which the owl vomits up.

The tail feathers of the crested argus pheasant can grow 1.7 metres/5.7 feet long. That's probably about as tall as one of your parents!

The American woodcock can only fly at 8 kilometres/5 miles per hour. That's about as fast as you can jog!

A *peregrine falcon* can fly speeds of 320 kilometres/200 miles per hour when diving through the air to catch its prey.

The brain of an ostrich is very small compared to its body size, making it one of the stupidest birds around.

Occasionally a chicken egg will produce two or more yolks. The most ever found in a single egg is nine!

A seagull has special glands that allow it to filter out the salt in seawater, allowing it to stray far away from land.

If a chicken has red *wattles* (the coloured pieces that hang down from their necks and heads), it will only produce brown eggs. If it has white wattles, it will only produce white eggs.

New York City is home to the world's largest urban population of peregrine falcons.

Ducks gather in groups to sleep. Those on the outer edge sleep with one eye open to keep watch for predators.

A male emperor penguin will go without food for up to 134 days while incubating the eggs laid by its female partner.

A group of owls is known as a 'parliament'.

All wild swans in England are the property of the Queen, who has an official swan keeper.

Birds that lay their eggs in the nests of other birds often check to see if their eggs are being cared for. If their eggs have been removed, the birds vandalize the nest, killing any other eggs or chicks.

Not all penguins live in cold climates – the Galápagos penguin lives near the equator in temperatures of up 29 degrees Celsius/ 84 degrees Fahrenheit.

The reef heron feeds on shellfish on the Great Barrier Reef, making a daily flight of 48 kilometres/30 miles from the Australian mainland. Even though the tide times vary, the heron always arrives at the exact moment that the tide goes out.

The *shrike* got its nickname of 'the butcher bird' from its habit of impaling its prey onto spikes to hold it still while devouring it.

Bald eagles can fly carrying 3.6 kilograms/8 pounds of food in their talons. Try carrying four bags of sugar to see how heavy it is!

A flamingo is pink because of the shrimp that it eats. A flamingo that doesn't eat shrimp will be almost white!

It takes 40 minutes to hard-boil an ostrich egg.

Woodpeckers slam their heads into trees at a rate of 20 pecks per second. A spongy area behind their beaks acts as a shock absorber and stops them from getting a headache.

You can hypnotize a chicken by repeatedly drawing a line on the ground in front of it. The chicken will stay in the same spot as long as you keep drawing the line!

The call of the Cape Barren goose sounds like the grunt of a pig.

The burrowing owl of North and South America makes its nest underground, and lines it with cow dung for warmth.

The roadrunner is actually a type of cuckoo.

The Arctic tern flies a round trip of 35,000 kilometres/21,750 miles a year, breeding in the Arctic in the northern summer and feeding in the Antarctic during the southern summer.

Experts have discovered that birds actually sing and chirp with regional accents!

Birds can't sweat! Up to three-quarters of the air a bird breathes is used for cooling its body down.

With the right wind conditions, an albatross can glide for six days without flapping its wings.

On 15 January 2009, a US Airways Flight crash-landed on the Hudson River in New York. A bird had been sucked into one of its engines causing power failure. Amazingly, no one was harmed!

Hummingbirds are the only birds that can fly backwards.

The strongest leather comes not from cows, but ostrich skin!

A hummingbird's legs are so light and flimsy that it can't walk; it can only perch or fly.

Owls are long-sighted, so they can't see things right in front of them very clearly.

Ravens have been known to undo velcro, untie knots in string and open zips to get at something they want.

Some Native American tribes believed that the roadrunner protected people against evil spirits.

A cockerel by the name of Mike was inexpertly beheaded in 1945 and lived for 18 months without his head! The Colorado farmer who owned Mike took him on tour and earned a small fortune.

Over 100 million birds die annually in the USA by accidentally crashing into glass windows. There are some pretty stupid birds out there!

There are 328 different species of parrot.

A toucan's beak is made of keratin, the same stuff from which your hair and nails are made.

Vultures are able to spot a carcass around the size of an average dog from 6.4 kilometres/4 miles away on open plains.

The mocking bird can perfectly imitate the songs of 40 different birds. Nobody knows what its Elvis impression is like, though...

Larger parrots, such as macaws and cockatoos, can live for more than 75 years.

If a bird is irritated by a human, it will direct its anger at other nearby birds as it would be too afraid to attack a human.

Around 190 species of bird have become extinct in the last 500 years.

The *scarlet tanager*, a songbird native to Illinois, USA, can eat as many as 2,100 gypsy moth caterpillars in one hour.

Chocolate is poisonous to parrots.

The *great hornbill* is able to consume as many as 150 figs in one meal!

Penguins have a special filter above their eyes. Excess water that they don't drink drips out of their bills. Sometimes they sneeze it out!

Guillemots are sea birds that roost in large groups. To help them tell their eggs apart, female guillemots lay eggs with very different patterns on the shells.

The *harpy eagle* is so large and powerful that it has been known to carry away a monkey in its talons.

Some sea birds, such as gulls and terns, have red oil in their eyes. This acts like a pair of sunglasses which protects their eyes from the glare of bright sunlight.

An albatross can sleep while it flies! It can doze while cruising at a terrifying 40 kilometres/25 miles per hour.

It is thought that up to 800,000 parrots are illegally captured each year to be sold as pets.

Ducks' feet contain no nerves or blood vessels. This means they never feel the cold when they swim in icy water.

To find water for their babies in the desert, sand grouse fly to an *oasis* (an isolated pool of water) up to 40 kilometres/25 miles away. They soak themselves in water and then go back to the nest where the chicks drink the water from their feathers.

The bald eagle is not really bald. It actually has white feathers on its head, neck, and tail. The 'bald' part comes from the Old English word *balde*, meaning 'white'.

In 1920's Britain, people used to clean their chimneys by dropping live chickens down them. The chickens would end up part-plucked and, if the chimney was still warm, part-cooked, too.

Wild turkeys can run at speeds of up to 40 kilometres/25 miles per hour.

Homing pigeons use the Earth's magnetic field to help them find their way home.

Hummingbird eggs are so small that your thumbnail would completely cover three of them.

Australian *lyrebirds* can perfectly imitate hundreds of sounds, including car alarms, chainsaws and even the clicking of tourists' cameras – learned from being photographed in the wild!

A man was fined AUS$25,000/£11,250 after hiding six rare birds' eggs in his underwear and trying to smuggle them out of Sydney airport.

Due to settlers arriving in America and destroying its habitat, the passenger pigeon went from being the most common bird in the world in 1810 to being extinct by 1914.

The *lappet-faced vulture* of Saudi Arabia is able to strip a small antelope carcass to the bone within 20 minutes.

The term 'swan song' comes from the ancient Greeks, who believed that a swan sang a song of death when its life was about to end.

The brown pelican has an extendable sac of skin at the base of its throat, which is capable of holding up to 11 litres/ 3 gallons of water.

If you fancy a chat, have a look for an African grey parrot – it has vocabulary of over 800 words!

Occasionally, a chicken egg can contain another complete egg inside it. This happens when an egg goes back up into a chicken, meets another egg on the way down and the second egg forms around the first one!

If a crow sees its reflection in a window it will sometimes fly at it repeatedly as it thinks it is a rival crow. It does this even though it hurts itself in the process!

When early Spanish explorers first encountered hummingbirds, they called them *joyas voladoras* meaning 'flying jewels.'

In 2005, a sparrow knocked over more than 23,000 dominoes that had been set up for a world record attempt in Leeuwarden, Holland. A clever back-up meant the record attempt of a 4-million domino rally was not completely lost.

A toucan's tongue is shorter than its impressive beak, so it can't use it to help get food into its mouth.

The *tailorbird* punches holes in leaves with its sharp bill and uses long grass to stitch them together to make a nest.

When the *Nuttall's Poorwill* of the USA hibernates in the winter, its heartbeat becomes so faint that it can't be felt.

Some birds swallow stones or grit to help break up the food in their stomachs, just like the dinosaurs did!

The kiwi bird of New Zealand has survived for more than 10,000 years despite the fact that it can't fly, lives in holes underground and is nearly blind!

The force of an eagle's talon is twice as powerful as a bullet being fired from a rifle.

Around 40 kamikaze birds crashed into windows and broke their necks in Vienna, Austria, after becoming drunk on fermented berries.

The now extinct passenger pigeon used to fly in flocks containing up to one billion birds. It would sometimes take days for a single flock to pass.

The sneaky *American wigeon* (a kind of duck) lets other ducks gather food…then swoops in and steals it!

The *cassowary bird* of New Guinea and Australia has a dagger-like 12-centimetre/5-inch long, razor sharp claw that can disembowel an enemy with a single kick.

Birds can eat berries that are highly poisonous to humans.

When police raided an elderly Swedish woman's apartment in 2007 they found that she had been sheltering 11 swans for more than five years!

Birds feed their babies by eating food for them! They go out, eat, then fly back to the nest and vomit up the meal into the babies' mouths. Lovely.

Because of the design of its beak, a flamingo always feeds with its head upside down.

Some parrot species fly over 800 kilometres/500 miles a day in the wild to forage for food.

The longest name of any bird is *griseotyrannus aurantioatrocristatus,* otherwise known as the crowned slaty flycatcher of South America.

If humans had the same *metabolism* (digestion rate) as hummingbirds, we would have to eat about 155,000 calories a day to stay alive – that's about 77 times the normal amount!

The phoenix fowl of Japan boasts the longest tail feathers of any bird, with some having tails that stretch to 10 metres/34 feet.

A four-legged duckling was born on a farm in Hampshire, England, in 2007. The farm owner named him Stumpy!

A colony of Adélie penguins can eat nearly 8 million kilograms/17.6 million pounds of krill and small fish every day.

Birds' eyes are fixed in their sockets, so they have to move their whole head to look at something. Try it yourself, keeping your eyes still!

A buzzard can see a small rodent from a height of 4,572 metres/15,000 feet. The highest point of Mount Kilimanjaro is 5,895 metres/19,341 feet!

During deep-sea dives, *gentoo penguins* reduce their heart rate from around 100 to just 20 beats per minute.

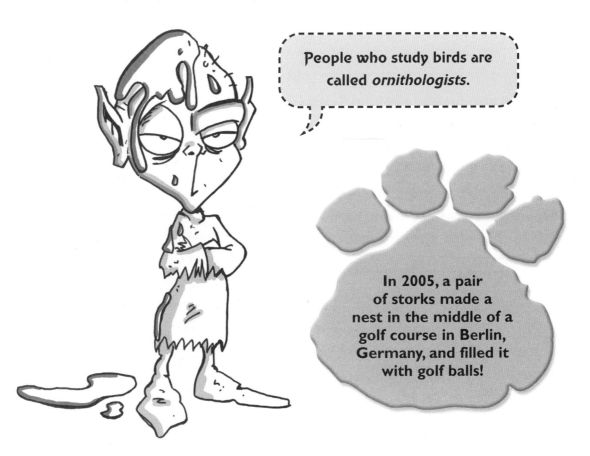

People who study birds are called *ornithologists*.

In 2005, a pair of storks made a nest in the middle of a golf course in Berlin, Germany, and filled it with golf balls!

Bald eagles can swim! They use an overhand movement of their wings that is similar to the butterfly stroke.

Peacocks do not have any coloured pigments to give them their amazing colours; the colours come from light reflecting off their transparent feathers.

Whooping cranes are born with blue eyes but they change to bright gold by the time they are six months old.

Alex the African grey parrot at Brandeis University, Massachusetts, USA, was taught to learn shapes, colours and materials and had the communication skills of a two-year old child. He could even tell lab assistants what he wanted them to change in his living environment!

Puffins' bills have sharp hooks on them that help to trap fish. One researcher noted seeing a puffin holding 62 fish at once in its bill.

Hooded Merganser ducklings from Canada gather together when in the water and form a tight compact group to protect them from predators. To hawks flying above them, they look just like a large swimming rodent.

Some birds kill parasites by putting ants between their feathers. The angry ants defend themselves by squirting formic acid, which kills the birds' parasites. Genius!

The hummingbird has a split tongue, just like a lizard!

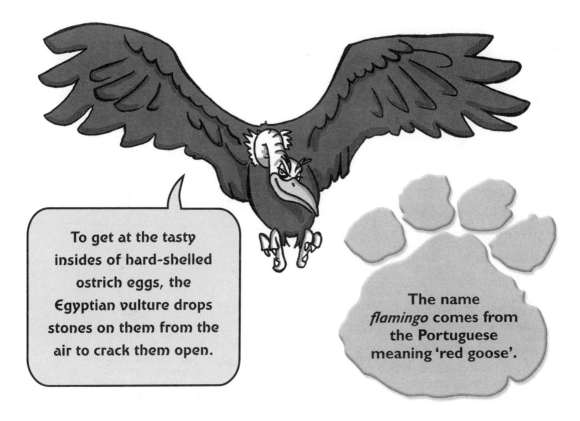

To get at the tasty insides of hard-shelled ostrich eggs, the Egyptian vulture drops stones on them from the air to crack them open.

The name *flamingo* comes from the Portuguese meaning 'red goose'.

Turkeys and chickens like to play with objects and toss them around. No word on the first chicken football team yet, though...

A *phalarope* (a type of water bird) likes to spin rapidly in water, like a spinning top. The spinning causes a small whirlpool that pulls tiny plankton to the surface of the water for it to feed on.

Only male canaries can sing.

The great tit produces its faeces in tiny sacs that it later removes from its nest. The average tit removes around 500 of these sacs from its nest each week – that's one busy little pooper!

Green herons have been known to drop berries, insects and other objects on to the surface of the water to attract fish. When a nosy fish comes to investigate, the heron strikes and bags himself a tasty snack.

When an ostrich living at London Zoo was examined for stomach problems, it was found to have swallowed a roll of camera film, a handkerchief, a piece of rope, a pencil, three gloves and six coins!

The Australian pelican has the longest beak in the world, growing up to 47 centimetres/18.5 inches long.

During the Middle Ages, swans and peacocks were often served as the main course of a Christmas dinner.

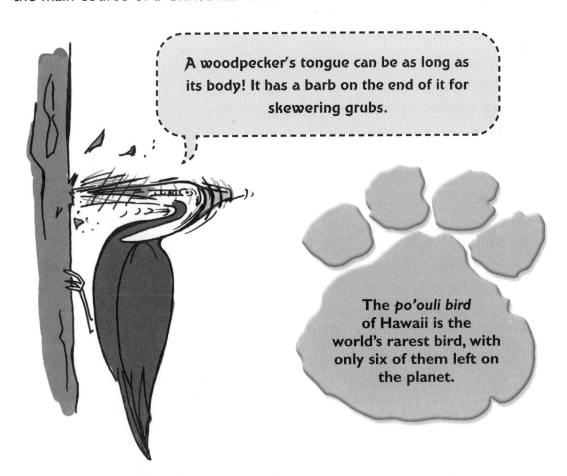

A woodpecker's tongue can be as long as its body! It has a barb on the end of it for skewering grubs.

The *po'ouli bird* of Hawaii is the world's rarest bird, with only six of them left on the planet.

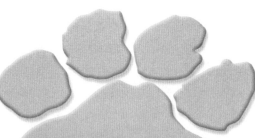

The largest wingspan ever recorded for a living bird was 3.63 metres/12.9 feet of a wandering albatross, caught in 1965.

The ancient Romans used to eat the rather stomach-turning delicacy of flamingo tongues. Yuck!

The most expensive book ever sold was a copy of John James Audobon's 1938 book *Birds of America*. It sold for a whopping US$8.8 million/£6.2 million.

When a flock of starlings perched on the minute hand of the famous London clock Big Ben in 1949, their combined weight quite literally stopped time!

It is estimated that two billion birds are killed in the USA each year by pet cats. Bad kitty!

Creepy Crawly
Facts

Tarantula spiders cannot spin webs.

A scorpion can go for a whole year without eating.

A mosquito can drink one and a half times its own weight in blood in a single meal.

Fearsome driver ants move in such massive colonies that they can strip the flesh from any animal they come across down to the bone. They have been known to completely devour wounded lions and crocodiles.

When it's time for dinner, a spider traps its prey before injecting it with a chemical that turns the bug's insides to mush. The spider then sucks out the liquid like a bug milkshake.

If salamander larvae detect tadpoles swimming in water around them, their bodies develop to become much stronger. They also grow flatter heads, making them killer predators.

The myth that garlic wards off vampires may not be true, but it does help repel mosquitoes.

Geckos clean their eyes using their tongues…a bit like windscreen wipers!

To defend their territory, guard termites sometimes make themselves explode to scare off attackers.

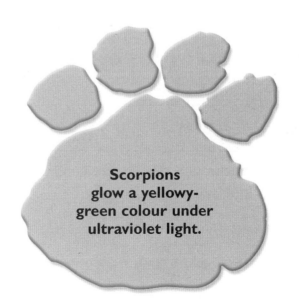

Scorpions glow a yellowy-green colour under ultraviolet light.

Instead of giving birth, a pregnant scorpion can sometimes reabsorb its babies back into its body.

The caterpillar of the *polyphemus moth* chomps its way through 86,000 times its own birth weight in food in the first 56 days of its life. That would be the same as a human baby munching through about 150,000 burgers!

The number of mosquitoes that hatch during the Arctic summer is so great that their swarms blot out the sun.

A cockroach can survive being frozen in a block of ice for two days.

Cockroaches taste with their feet.

The Australian bulldog ant can kill a human in 15 minutes by clinging on to a person's skin with its strong jaws and stinging over and over again.

Only female mosquitos drink human blood. They do it to get the protein they need to lay eggs.

Queen termites lay an egg every second for up to 50 years.

A cockroach can 'hiss' by squeezing air out of tiny holes in its body. It can be heard up to 3.5 metres/12 feet away.

A fly's eye blinks at five times the rate of a human eye. If a fly watched a movie, it would see it as a series of still photographs.

The snow scorpion that lives in the Alps is used to such low temperatures that even holding one in your hand will cause it to die from heat exhaustion.

Slugs like drinking beer! Some gardeners leave traps for them, so that the slugs get drunk and drown.

The giant African land snail can grow to 39 centimetres/15 inches and weigh 900 grams/ 2 pounds.

The minimum temperature a grasshopper needs to be able to hop is 17 degrees Celsius/62 degrees Fahrenheit. Any colder, and its powerful muscles are too stiff to lift it off the ground.

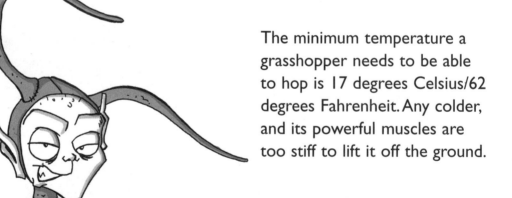

Astronauts lose consciousness at 12 times the pressure of Earth's gravity. A cockroach can withstand up to ten times that amount.

A patch of rainforest soil around the size of this book can contain 10,000 mosquito eggs.

A cockroach can live for a week after having its head cut off. It only dies through starvation.

The female black widow spider eats the male after mating, sometimes eating up to 25 partners a day. Now that's a real man-eater!

Some leeches have 300 teeth, with 100 in each of their three blood-sucking jaws.

A leech will only finish sucking blood when it is five times its original size.

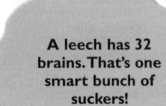

A leech has 32 brains. That's one smart bunch of suckers!

The world's population of termites expels up to 79 billion kilograms/176 billion pounds of gas every year. That's 34 times more than the human population!

Flea larvae like to eat their parents' faeces...or each other!

A flea can jump 30,000 times without stopping.

A sausage fly is not actually a fly, but a male driver ant with a bloated, sausage-shaped abdomen.

Ants can carry a load around 100 times their own body weight.

There are 100 million more insects on earth than there are humans.

Insects eat 10 per cent of the world's food supply each year. You'll never catch them pushing a trolley round the supermarket, though!

The light from six large fireflies is enough to read by. Pretty handy on a summer's evening...

The Japanese beetle, found in Canada and the USA, can eat through a human eardrum.

A grasshopper can jump to 500 times its own height.

Relative to their size, fleas can accelerate 50 times faster than the space shuttle!

A cockroach can hold its breath underwater for up to 40 minutes.

When a mosquito bites you, it's the enzymes in its saliva that causes you to itch, not the bite itself.

Wasps that feed on fermented fruit occasionally get drunk and pass out.

A slug has four noses.

The record for the world's heaviest spider was a giant bird-eating spider found in Suriname in 1965. It weighed 122 grams/4 ounces. That's about the same as a large apple!

10,000 new species of insect are discovered every year.

Ants recognize other ants from the same colony by their smell.

To build their nests, weaver ants line up in a row and use their *mandibles* (jaws) to pull nearby leaves together. They then squeeze their larvae so that they produce a fine thread of silk, which is used to 'stitch' the nest together!

Mosquitoes are strongly attracted to people who have recently eaten bananas.

Locusts can fly for 20 hours without stopping.

There are at least 3,700 species of beetle in Britain alone. Just hope they don't all pop round for a visit at once...

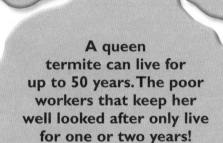

A queen termite can live for up to 50 years. The poor workers that keep her well looked after only live for one or two years!

Spiders like to snack! They keep extra bugs wrapped up in their web as tasty treats between large meals.

An earthworm tastes with its whole body – it has taste receptors spread all over it. Every time you pick one up they are getting a little taste of you, too!

Earthworms have ten hearts! They help them to breathe, as the veins closest to the skin take in oxygen.

The slime produced by snails is so protectively slimy that a snail could crawl along the edge of a razor blade without cutting itself.

Snails can sleep for up to three years in one single snooze.

Never squash a *yellowjacket wasp* near its nest. A dying yellowjacket releases a *pheromone* (chemical) that alerts its comrades to danger. In less than 15 seconds, any wasps within a 4.5-metre/15-foot radius will swarm to the dying wasp's aid.

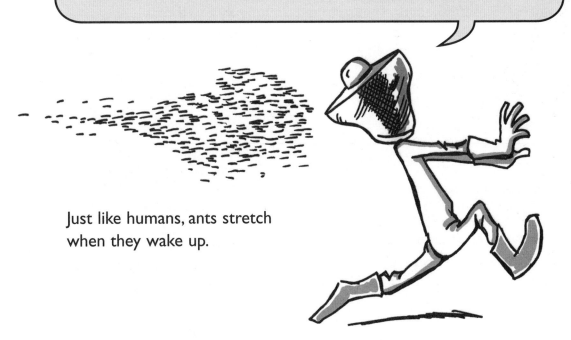

Just like humans, ants stretch when they wake up.

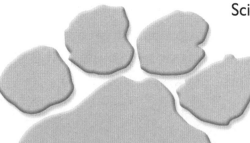

Butterflies that fly at night have ears on their wings so that they can listen out for predators.

Scientists have taught tricks to fish, worms, cockroaches, ants and even snails, but never flies. Scientists aren't sure if flies are thick, or just want nothing to do with humans.

Ants can detect movements through 5 centimetres/2 inches of earth.

The *giant gippsland earthworm* of Australia can grow up to 4.5 metres/15 feet in length. That's almost as long as a python.

Adult earwigs can float in water for up to 24 hours without dying.

There are 35,000 species of spider but only 27 are known to be deadly to humans.

A dragonfly has two sets of wings that can flap independently of each other. Their front wings can be going up while their back ones are going down!

In summer, Inuit people from the Arctic cover themselves with a thick layer of mud to avoid being attacked by fierce biting flies.

Eastern European peasants used to make wound dressings out of spiders' webs. Spider silk has antiseptic properties, so it wasn't such a bad idea.

Tarantulas can live for up to 30 years.

Worker bees have 5,500 lenses in each eye. These allow the bee to see ultraviolet light that is invisible to the human eye.

There are 4,300 known species of ladybird in the world. They're not just red – they can be yellow, blue or even multi-coloured!

A poisonous spider called the *false widow* travelled to England in a bunch of bananas. Warm weather has allowed it to survive, so there are now tens of thousands running wild in just ten years.

Head lice can change appearance to match the colour of the hair in which they are living.

It has been calculated that an ant's brain has more processing power than the computer that controlled the first *Apollo* space missions.

The sting of a tropical cone snail can be fatal to a human being. Luckily, they live underwater so you should be safe in your garden...

Cockroaches breed so fast that if a single pair reproduced for a year, with all their babies reproducing as well, there would be ten million of them altogether.

Baby *periodical cicadas* (similar to locusts) live underground for up to 17 years. When they finally emerge as adults, they only live for three weeks. What a lot of time for nothing!

Eighty per cent of all living things are *nematode worms* – simple worms found everywhere including salt and fresh water, soil and inside plants and animals.

The *necrophorus beetle* uses the fur of dead animals to build its nest.

You can't feel the bite of a leech because it produces a natural painkiller before latching on. How thoughtful...

The tarantula hawk is actually a wasp! The female wasp attacks and paralyzes a tarantula spider before laying an egg in its body. The hatched wasp then eats the tarantula alive as its first meal.

The fat-tailed scorpion is responsible for most human deaths from scorpion stings. Although its venom is less toxic than that of the deathstalker scorpion, it injects more into its victim.

The Pharaoh ant loves to feast on human wounds and bloody bandages. It's a regular visitor to the hospital…

Locusts travel in swarms of up to 80 million.

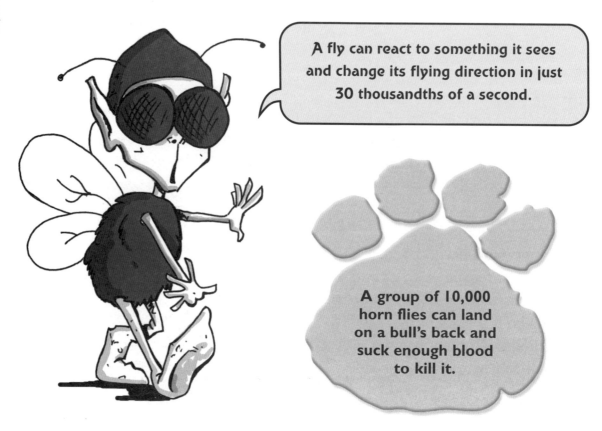

A fly can react to something it sees and change its flying direction in just 30 thousandths of a second.

A group of 10,000 horn flies can land on a bull's back and suck enough blood to kill it.

There are approximately 10,000 flies to every single human being on the planet.

In order to crawl into tiny cracks, cockroaches can flatten their bodies to just a little thicker than a piece of paper.

Some species of dragonfly can travel at around 48 kilometres/30 miles per hour. Notice how fast that is next time you're in a car!

If you weighed all of the people who live in the USA, and all of the earthworms in the USA, the earthworms would weigh 50 times more!

The guts of the African *N'gwa caterpillar* are so poisonous that tribesmen use them to tip their spears and arrowheads.

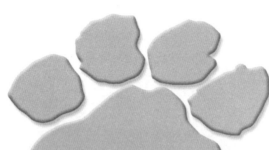

A clothing moth's favourite meal is a dirty woolly jumper. The more sweat, food and oils there are, the better.

If you cut a leech in half while it is feeding, it will carry on sucking even though the blood will spurt out of the severed end of its body.

Goliath bird-eating spiders are so huge that they can grow to the size of a dinner plate. The largest known example was found in Venezuela in 1965 and measured 28 centimetres/11 inches across. That's almost as long as your school ruler!

Spiders' silk is stronger than steel. If you stretched equal-sized threads of steel and spiders' silk, the steel thread would break first.

If cut in half in the right place, a healthy earthworm can grow a new head or tail. Of course, the worm might think there is no 'right place' to be cut in half!

To help transport their communication sounds, some crickets burrow tunnels in the earth, which that act as megaphones. The sound can be heard from 610 metres/2,000 feet away.

Between 20–30 July 1874, a swarm of Rock Mountain locusts flew over Nebraska, covering an area approximately 515,000 square kilometres/198,600 square miles.

From 4 litres/1 gallon of nectar, a bee could fly for 6.5 million kilometres/4 million miles. Now that's fuel efficiency!

There are 70,000 different types of slug and snail in the world.

If two flies were left to reproduce for a year, without threat from predators, the resulting mass of flies would be the size of planet Earth!

A German cockroach can survive for more than a month without food but only two weeks without water.

In just 2.5 square kilometres/1 square mile of rural land, you could find more insects than there are humans on the entire planet!

To keep their young safe and dry during floods, a colony of tropical ants will roll themselves into a huge living ball, which safely floats in water.

A honeybee travels an average of 1,500 round trips in order to produce five teaspoons of honey.

The mating call of the male cicada can be heard as far away as 400 metres/1,320 feet. That's one noisy little bug.

Honeybees have regional accents! Bees from different places use different dances and movements to communicate.

A fly's wings beat around 180 times a second!

The blood consumed in a single meal can keep a leech alive for up to nine months.

A scorpion can be frozen in a block of ice for three weeks and then crawl away unharmed.

Flies can taste what they are standing on because of the 1,500 tiny taste hairs on their feet.

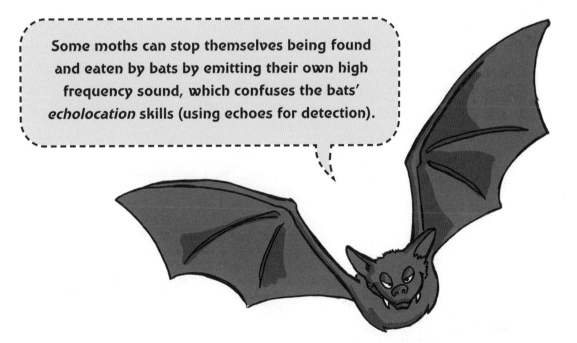

Some moths can stop themselves being found and eaten by bats by emitting their own high frequency sound, which confuses the bats' *echolocation* skills (using echoes for detection).

Head lice have two mouthparts: one cuts the skin and sucks up blood; the other pumps out a chemical that helps to stop the blood clotting.

To land on your ceiling, a fly has to grab hold with its front legs then do a somersault in order to bring its back legs into contact with the ceiling.

Blowflies are the first kind of insect attracted to a carcass (the body of a dead animal) following its death.

There are approximately 40–45,000 bees in an average beehive. Remember that next time you go looking for honey…

The goliath beetle is the world's biggest bug, weighing in at 99 grams/3.5 ounces and being 11.5 centimetres/4.5 inches long.

A housefly's feet are ten million times more sensitive to taste than a human tongue is.

The Queen Alexandra's birdwing butterly from New Guinea is the largest known butterfly in the world, with a wingspan of approximately 27.9 centimetres/11 inches.

Despite the popular myth, a daddy long legs' venom is not dangerous to humans. It has never been studied in depth as the poor arachnid cannot open its jaws wide enough to be able to bite humans.

A scorpion can withstand up to 200 times the amount of radiation that would kill a human.

A dragonfly lives for up to seven years but only spends between three and four months of its life as a flying adult.

The jumping ability of a flea is the equivalent of an adult human jumping over a 25–storey building.

Driver ants kill their victims not by poison or venom, but by slashing at them with their pincers. They do it in such great numbers that their prey eventually bleeds to death from thousands of tiny cuts.

Some types of *botfly* lay their eggs on the abdomens of other blood-sucking insects such as fleas or ticks. When they hatch, the baby botflies burrow into the skin of the animal and suck the poor victim dry as their first meal.

The St Andrew's cross spider is so named because it rests in its web with its legs outstretched in an X shape.

Because maggots have no teeth, they ooze *ferment* (saliva) from of their mouths to liquidize their food before sucking it up.

A monarch butterfly was released near Ontario in Canada and was recovered four months later in Angangueo, Mexico. The straight-line distance between the two sites is 3,433 kilometres/2,133 miles.

Greenfly are actually born pregnant with clones (exact copies of themselves) which they later give birth to. Weird…

When threatened, the devil's coach horse beetle curls its tail upwards like a scorpion and lets out an unpleasant odour from both its mouth and bottom!

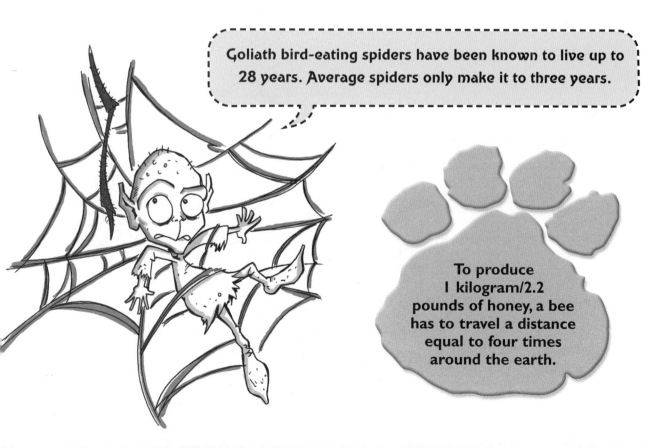

Goliath bird-eating spiders have been known to live up to 28 years. Average spiders only make it to three years.

To produce 1 kilogram/2.2 pounds of honey, a bee has to travel a distance equal to four times around the earth.

You can find out the temperature outside (in degrees Fahrenheit) by counting a cricket's chirps for 13 seconds and adding 40.

The *patu marplesi* of Samoa is the world's smallest spider, growing to a total of 0.004 centimetres/ 0.0017 inches. How big is that? Smaller than the full stop at the end of this sentence.

The *anopheles mosquito* is thought to be responsible for half of all non-accidental human deaths in history since the Stone Age. It is the primary carrier of the deadly disease *malaria*.

The weight of all the insects eaten by spiders every year is more than the total weight of the human population.

Ants, termites, grasshoppers and wasps were all around during the time of the dinosaurs.

Scientists have recently discovered that some large insect colonies, such as those of cockroaches and bees, use a voting system to decide where to make their next home.

If you weighed all the ants in the world, they would equal roughly the weight of all the humans in the world.

The female Jewel wasp can turn a cockroach into a 'zombie' by stinging it in the head. The cockroach lies paralyzed while the wasp lays its eggs in its body, only dying when the hatched wasp larva chews its way out of the cockroach's stomach.

When taking off, flies jump up and backwards. If you want to swat a fly, come at it from behind and there is a good chance it will simply leap into your hand as it tries to take off.

Fireflies are not really flies – they are a type of beetle.

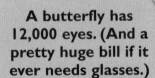

A butterfly has 12,000 eyes. (And a pretty huge bill if it ever needs glasses.)

Despite popular belief, the bite of a black widow spider is rarely fatal. The amount of venom injected is not enough to actually kill a healthy adult human. Less than 1 per cent of bites actually lead to death.

The only insect that can turn its head a full 360 degrees is the preying mantis.

The largest cockroaches in the world are the colossus cockroaches of Columbia. They can grow to be bigger than the palm of your hand.

Africanized bees have been known to pursue an enemy for more than half a kilometre/quarter of a mile. Never upset an Africanized bee unless you have a very fast car...

Wet and Wild
Facts

The only creature known to have just one eye is the corepod. It is a tiny crustacean that swims around in groups of up to one trillion members.

If a shark gets turned onto its back, it goes into a state of paralysis for up to 15 minutes.

The tentacles of a lion's mane jellyfish can reach up to 60 metres/200 feet away from its body.

The vampire squid has the largest eyes of any animal in relation to its body size. If it was the size of a human, it would have eyes the size of table tennis bats!

A shark can sense even a small amount of blood in water over 1 kilometre/half a mile away.

Leatherback turtles have spines in their throats! They stop their favourite snack of jellyfish from sliding back out of their mouths.

If an octopus loses a tentacle, it can grow a new one!

The deep sea gulper eel can open its mouth so wide that its jaws can bend back at a 180 degree angle. This allows it to eat fish larger than itself.

Halfway between a tadpole and a lizard, the *axolotl* is a species of amphibian that is native to a single lake in Mexico. In extreme cases, if the water level drops too far, an *axolotl* can grow legs and become a land creature.

A special cap on the end of a stingray's tail will break off when it attacks its prey. This allows even more poison to flow out into its victim's wound.

Sharks have special organs in their snouts that detect the electric fields produced by other living creatures.

Even after it has been cut off, an octopus tentacle will carry on wriggling for some time.

Electric eels can deliver a shock of 500 volts to stun their prey into submission. The electricity supplied to your home is only 240 volts!

The tentacles of the deadly box jellyfish contain tiny harpoons which inject poison into its unlucky victim.

The anglerfish lives in the darkest depths of the sea and has a glowing blob, like a little lantern, dangling in front of its head!

If pulled out of the sea by fishermen, the quick change in water pressure makes the gases inside a Pacific grenadier fish expand. Its stomach pops out of its mouth as a result!

The jaws of a snapping turtle are so powerful that they can rip off a human finger.

The viperfish can move all its internal organs towards its tail when it needs to make room for a large meal.

A group of jellyfish is called a 'smack'.

An octopus will sometimes eat its own tentacles, and even its own body, if it becomes extremely stressed.

Green sea turtles can stay underwater for up to five hours. To achieve this, they slow their heart rate to help conserve oxygen, with up to nine minutes between heartbeats.

If you spread them out, the tentacles of an Arctic jellyfish would stretch over 15 tennis courts.

Some types of octopus contain a poison that instantly kills any creature that eats them.

Dolphins sleep with one eye open! They shut down each side of their brain separately to have a rest.

If you kept a goldfish in a darkened room for long enough, it would eventually turn white.

A female tiger shark carries several babies during pregnancy but only gives birth to one. In the womb, the strongest baby eats the others until it is the only one left.

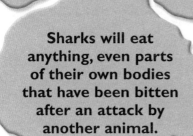

Sharks will eat anything, even parts of their own bodies that have been bitten after an attack by another animal.

A starfish can turn its stomach inside out by pushing it through its mouth.

An oyster can change its sex several times during its life!

You could power two fridges with the electricity produced by a single electric eel.

A shark will drown if it stops swimming. It has to keep water moving through its gills at all times, so can never properly sleep.

A killifish embryo can survive in mud, with no water or oxygen, for more than 60 days.

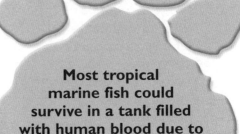

Most tropical marine fish could survive in a tank filled with human blood due to the amount of oxygen it contains.

The heart of a blue whale only beats four to eight times a minute. (A human heart averages around 75 beats per minute.)

Instead of black ink, some species of deep sea squid squirt a cloud of glowing luminous ink to distract predators in the dark depths of the ocean.

If a dolphin loses its tail, scientists can attach an artificial rubber tail made from the same material used to make Formula 1 tyres. It's proven to work as well as the real thing!

When a baby octopus is born, it is about the size of a flea.

To help them navigate in dark or murky water, fish have a movement sensor in their bodies called a *lateral line*. If you look at a fish closely, you'll be able to see two faint lines running down its side.

If you catch a sturgeon (the fish that produces caviar) in British waters, it is considered to be the property of the Queen.

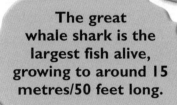

The great whale shark is the largest fish alive, growing to around 15 metres/50 feet long.

Ancient Greek dentists used the venom from a stingray's spine as an anaesthetic.

So far, over 35,000 species of fish have been identified, compared with only 4,600 species of mammal.

The robber crab got its nickname from its habit of stealing shiny things like pots and pans from people's houses!

When fully grown, the Philippine goby fish is only 0.7 centimetres/ 0.3 inches long. That's smaller than your little fingernail!

Little is known about the megamouth shark as it was first discovered by scientists in 1976. Only three photographs of it in its natural habitat exist in the entire world.

The pistol shrimp got its name from the loud banging noise it makes with its claws in order to surprise its prey.

The largest lake trout ever found weighed 46.3 kilograms/102 pounds. That's about the same weight as some horse jockeys!

Less than 0.1 per cent of the earth's water is fresh water, yet it is home to a whopping 40 per cent of all fish species.

The most toxic natural poison in the world actually comes from a piece of coral. The poison of the *palythoa* can kill a rabbit with only a 25-nanogram injection; 4 micrograms can kill a human. Death occurs within minutes and there is no known antidote.

The washed up empty egg case of a dogfish, skate or shark is called a *mermaid's purse*.

A jellyfish is 95 per cent water – the same as a cucumber! Not as nice in a salad though...

In just one year, lemon sharks grow more than 24,000 new teeth. That's a full set every two weeks! Who needs to bother with brushing?

When it has eaten as much as it can, a barracuda will herd any remaining fish that it has not eaten into shallow water. It guards them until it is ready to eat again.

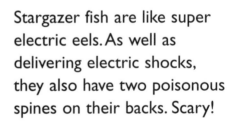

A glassfish is completely transparent, so you can see all its bones and internal organs without cutting it open.

Stargazer fish are like super electric eels. As well as delivering electric shocks, they also have two poisonous spines on their backs. Scary!

Some fish can get seasick.

All yellowmouth grouper fish are born female. As they grow they eventually change into males, but only a small percentage ever survive long enough to make the change.

The slime eel, also known as the hagfish, feeds on dead and dying fish at the bottom of the sea. After slipping through its mouth or eye socket, the eel eats the insides of the dead creature, leaving only a bag of skin and bones at the end.

Tuna fish swim constantly for their entire lives. Over 15 years, a single tuna will cover a distance of around 1.6 million kilometres/1 million miles.

The long horn of the narwhal is actually an extended tooth! Its other name, 'unicorn of the sea', isn't exactly correct…

Octopuses have been known to remove the stinging tentacles from jellyfish and use them as weapons.

A dying barracuda fish will gorge itself on anything that will make its flesh poisonous, such as small creatures and plants. That way, anything that eats the barracuda after it dies will also be killed. Nasty!

The parrotfish can make itself a kind of mucus sleeping bag, which masks its smell from predators and helps keep parasites away.

The Barents Sea is teeming with monster kamchatka crabs, after they were introduced in the 1960s to provide a fishing source for Russian fisherman. The gigantic crustaceans can measure more than 1 metre/3 feet from claw to claw.

A female cod can lay up to 9 million eggs in a single pregnancy.

Goldfish are the only animals that can see in both ultraviolet and infrared light.

Lizardfish have sharp teeth on their tongues!

A catfish has ten times as many taste buds as a human.

Fishing nets are designed with holes in the bottom to let dolphins and other big creatures to escape. The nets work because fish such as haddock are not brainy enough to realize they can swim downwards!

Some sharks can detect the smell of fish at concentrations as low as one part in ten billion.

Lobsters are scared of octopuses. Even the sight of one is enough to make a lobster freeze in horror.

The desert pupfish, found in isolated pools in Death Valley, USA, can survive in water three times saltier than the ocean. It can also endure temperatures of more than 38 degrees Celsius/100 degrees Farenheit.

The viperfish catches its prey by swimming straight towards its target and impaling (spearing) it on its huge teeth.

The coconut crab can climb trees up to 6 metres/19 feet high to grab coconuts from the tops!

A *quahog clam* found off the coast of Iceland in 2007 has been identified as being between 405 and 410 years old, making it the oldest animal ever discovered. It was a baby when Elizabeth I was on the throne in England (1558–1603), and was nearly 350 years old by the end of World War II!

In 2001, a giant catfish in a park lake in Germany became known as 'Kuno the killer' after it jumped out and ate a Dachshund puppy – whole!

A sperm whale can dive to depths of 2 kilometres/1.25 miles.

Some of the items found inside sharks' stomachs include a horse's head, a porcupine, parts of bicycles and cars, a sheep, a chicken coop – and even a suit of armour with the remains of a French soldier inside!

The *flying gurnard* swims in water, walks on land and flies through the air...and most unbelievable of all, it's a fish!

Some health spas use *garra rufa* fish to treat skin problems. People sit in shallow pools filled with the fish, then wait for their dead skin and scabby bits to be nibbled away!

Sharks' skins are covered in sharp, tooth-like scales called *denticles*, which feel like sandpaper to touch.

Despite its beautiful looks, the flesh of the *blue tang* fish is actually poisonous if eaten by humans or other fish.

The *crevalle jack* (a type of fish) is capable of producing croaking sounds by grinding its teeth together while releasing gas from its swim bladder.

A whale shark can filter up to 400,000 gallons/1.5 million litres of water an hour when feeding.

More than 50 per cent of all creatures brought up from the deep sea by scientists are unknown species.

Octopuses have three hearts! Two pump blood through its gills to help it breathe while the third pumps blood around the rest of its body.

The slender giant moray eel has been known to grow to nearly 4 metres/13 feet in length.

When a turtle eats a Portuguese man-of-war jellyfish, the jellyfish releases a smell that attracts sharks. It's the jellyfish's way of getting revenge on the turtle!

The largest giant squid ever caught was a whopping 18.2 metres/60 feet long and weighed 907 kilograms/2,000 pounds. Its body was so enormous that *calamari rings* (squid rings) made from it would have been the size of tractor tyres!

If you're attacked by a moray eel, the only way to get away is to kill it by cutting off its head and breaking its jaws. It won't let go while it's alive.

The *tridacna clam* has been known to grow up to 1.2 metres/4 feet long and weigh up to 227 kilograms/500 pounds. Not bad for a clam!

The arteries of the massive blue whale are so huge that a human baby could crawl through them.

The *Asian climbing perch* can 'walk' on land in search of water when its water source dries up. It uses its fins and tail to pull itself along the ground.

Whales can't actually move their eyeballs. In order to see, a whale has to move its entire body. Try it yourself... not easy!

When under attack, a hagfish produces slimy mucus which makes the water around it turn into jelly that is impossible for predators to swim through.

Using sonar equipment, scientists can detect the sounds made by fin whales and blue whales from up to 850 kilometres/350 miles away.

The teeth of a viperfish are half the length of its head, so it can't close its mouth! It has to open its jaws very wide in order to swallow.

A blue whale's tongue can weigh the same as an elephant.

Killer whales have been known to attack sharks by launching themselves into their prey's stomach like a torpedo. The force of the impact can even cause the victim shark to explode.

The *cosmopolitan sailfish* can swim faster than a cheetah can run! It can swim 109 kilometres/68 miles per hour – that's 9 kilometres/6 miles faster than a cheetah's top speed.

A scallop has about 100 eyes around the edge of its shell. Very handy for spotting approaching predators...

Some fish live so deep in the sea that sunlight can't reach them and they live in complete darkness. Many species make their own light using a chemical reaction called *bioluminescence*.

The *mola mola*, or *ocean sunfish*, lays up to 5,000,000 eggs at one time.

The longest whale ever found was a blue whale, measuring just over 33 metres/110 feet. That's the length of nine family cars end to end!

Whales sometimes beach themselves (get stranded on land) and are unable to swim back into the sea. If a whale is stranded its distress call brings others to help, sometimes leading to whole schools of whales being beached at once.

The *lungfish* can live out of water for as long as four years!

Sharks and rays are the only animals on the planet that are immune to cancer. Scientists believe this may be something to do with their skeletons, which are made of cartilage rather than bone.

The ostrich is often credited with laying the largest eggs, but the world's largest egg was actually laid by a whale shark! The 36-centimetre/14-inch egg was found in the Gulf of Mexico in 1953.

In an effort to get them to mate, a German aquarium plays love songs to its sharks!

Even though there are more than 250 known species of shark in the world, only about 18 are actually dangerous to humans. Most attacks are accidents when a shark mistakes a human for another animal.

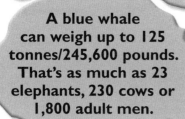

A blue whale can weigh up to 125 tonnes/245,600 pounds. That's as much as 23 elephants, 230 cows or 1,800 adult men.

Seahorses can see in two directions at once, as their eyes can move independently of each other.

A sea slug can eat a *hyrdroid* (an underwater stinging nettle) without being stung. The stinging chemical is absorbed into its skin and then stings anything that tries to eat the slug. Clever!

The moray eel has two sets of teeth in its throat; the first set bites the eel's prey, while the second set moves up into the eel's mouth and locks on more tightly. The first set then moves to pull the prey down the eel's throat.

The *lamprey*, an eel-like creature, has no jaws. To eat, it attaches its sucker mouth to another fish then literally sucks all the fluids out of it, killing the fish by sucking it dry.

A starfish doesn't have a brain. An extremely complex nerve system called the *nerve plexus* controls its arms instead.

If you place a *sole* (a type of flat fish) on a chessboard, it will take just four minutes to change its body colour to match the square pattern of the board.

The largest great white shark ever caught measured 11.2 metres/37 feet and weighed 10.8 tons/24,000 pounds. It was found in a herring weir in New Brunswick, Canada, in 1930.

A baby blue whale drinks 227 litres/50 gallons of milk from its mother every day.

Some fish in Antarctica have a natural antifreeze in their bodies which makes their blood appear white instead of red.

The *mimic octopus* can change its shape and body colour in order to scare off predators. It has been known to make itself look like a very convincing sea snake.

Electric rays have two special kidney-shaped organs in their bodies which generate and store electricity – just like a battery!

While most fish use gas-filled swim bladders for *buoyancy* (staying afloat), a shark uses its liver for the same purpose.

Piranhas' teeth are so strong that they can bite neatly through a steel fishing hook.

Turtles live on every continent except Antarctica.

Some female bony fish can produce babies without a partner. The baby is a clone of its mother.

Because whales are so slow-moving, they often have barnacles attached to them. They can comfortably carry up to 454 kilograms/1,000 pounds of barnacles around with them!

Male seahorses become pregnant! The babies grow for three weeks in a pouch before the male gives birth to up to 200 of them over 72 hours. The effort leaves him drained of colour – not surprisingly!

Because of the design of their jaws, fish can't actually chew – they swallow most of their food whole.

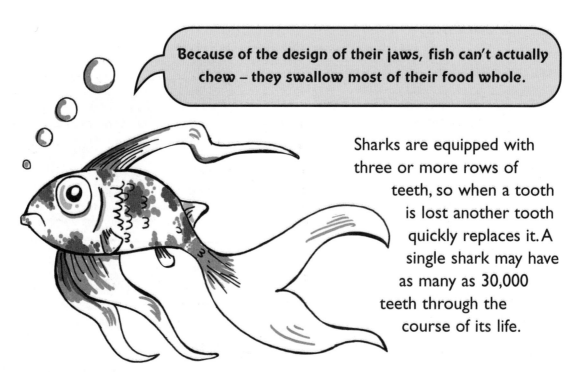

Sharks are equipped with three or more rows of teeth, so when a tooth is lost another tooth quickly replaces it. A single shark may have as many as 30,000 teeth through the course of its life.

The black drum (a type of fish found in the Gulf of Mexico) gets its name from its ability to use its large swim bladder to produce croaking or drumming sounds.

Glass eels are always determined to get to their destination and have been known to climb up the wet walls of dams to get around an obstacle in their way.

Giant sea stars are starfish that can have an arm span of more than 60 centimetres/24 inches! They can be brown, green, red or orange.

In 2003, the Australian navy boarded an Indonesian ship that was drifting off the coast and found no sign of the crew or indications of an emergency. The only thing they found onboard was 3 tonnes/6,614 pounds of rotting mackerel and tuna.

Catfish have tastebuds on their *barbels* (fleshy whiskers) which means that they can taste things by simply brushing up against them.

Walruses fill an inflatable throat pouch called a *pharyngeal* with air to keep them afloat while they sleep.

Despite not having a male partner, a hammerhead shark gave birth in a zoo in Nebraska, USA, in 2001. The female shark used a type of reproduction called *parthenogenesis* in order to keep the species alive when no male sharks are available.

Great white sharks have a bite three times more powerful than that of an African lion.

Some grouper fish are so huge that when they open their mouths they create a suction that pulls prey into their mouths.

Odobenus rosmarus, the scientific name for a walrus, is Latin for 'tooth-walking sea-horse'.

Why keep normal pet goldfish when a Taiwanese company has made a fish that glows different colours! By injecting a protein extracted from jellyfish, the super-fish glows gold under normal light and a variety of different colours under aquarium lights.

A team of 47 football-playing crocodiles are owned by Erroberto Piza Rios of Ixtapa, Mexico. Their ball control skills are impressive, but they do make some nasty tackles…

In 2006, Blake Fessenden was jet skiing on the Suwanee River in Florida, USA, when a sturgeon jumped out of the river and knocked him unconscious. That's one mean fish!

When returning to their spawning ground at the top of the Orrin Falls in Scotland, salmon have to make a huge leap of 3.7 metres/12 feet into the air!

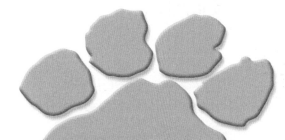

The total weight of all the *krill* (shrimp-like crustaceans) in the Antarctic is more than the total weight of all the humans on the planet.

The archerfish likes to lurk near the surface of the water before spitting well-targeted jets to knock down passing flying insects and eating them.

The *long-nosed chimaera* fish lives in the deep sea around South Africa at depths of 2438 metres/8,000 feet and has a nose shaped like a fighter plane. Don't get too close though, as a single touch from its spine is enough to kill a human.

The closest living relatives to the manatee are actually elephants and aardvarks.

The collective name for a group of herring is a 'siege'.

The grey seal's scientific name, *Halichoerus grypus*, comes from the Greek meaning 'hook-nosed sea pig'.

Crazy Creature
Facts

A rat's teeth grow continuously during its life. If it didn't keep chewing, its lower teeth would eventually grow through its top jaw and through the roof of its mouth.

Rats are so tough that they can fall from a five-storey building and walk away unharmed.

A plague of *flying foxes* (fruit bats) has been known to consume an entire orchard in just one night!

Anteaters, armadillos, bats, duck-billed platypuses, whales, dolphins and porpoises are all immune to getting lice.

A vampire bat can drink half its own body weight in blood every day.

Rats' teeth are so strong that they can bite through wood, metal and electric cables. Not good news if they're in your attic, then…

During mating competitions, Montana mountain goats can butt heads so hard that the shock can cause their hooves to fall off.

An elephant's trunk is so useful that it can pluck a single blade of grass from the ground.

Vampire bats are surprisingly thoughtful. If a bat is too ill to go out and feed, another bat will suck blood all night, come home, and vomit it up over the poorly bat so that it doesn't miss out on a meal. How kind!

Three-toed sloths often appear green. They move so slowly that algae grows on their fur!

If you are getting eaten by something big, green and full of teeth, the chances are it's a crocodile; alligators don't like the taste of humans.

Some chameleons have a sticky goo-covered lump on their tongues which helps them to catch insects.

Most hamsters blink with one eye at a time.

The skin under a polar bear's white fur is actually black!

Crocodiles can't chew their food. Instead, they hold their prey and then twist their bodies and teeth around it to tear off chunks of flesh.

The bite of a Komodo dragon isn't poisonous, but there are so many bacteria in their mouths – growing in rotten meat between their teeth – that a bite from one often leads to blood poisoning and death.

To keep themselves cool, some tortoises urinate on their back legs. The evaporating liquid helps take away body heat.

A python can live for a whole year without eating anything.

Just a single bat can eat between 3,000 and 7,000 mosquitoes in a night. A colony of 500 of the flying fiends can munch their way through a quarter of a million bugs in an hour.

The longest recorded flight for a chicken is 13 seconds.

The contents of a sloth's stomach can take up to a month to be digested completely. That's a lot of mouldy twigs and berries…

The African pygmy mouse finds water by stacking pebbles in front of its burrow and drinking the dew from them in the morning.

Beavers have a set of transparent eyelids that they use to protect their eyes when they swim underwater.

It takes 3,000 cows to supply enough leather for a year's supply of footballs for the USA's National Football League.

An elephant has four functional teeth, each one being 30 centimetres/12 inches long. They are replaced six times in its lifetime, but after the last replacement the elephant can no longer feed properly.

Meerkats are immune to many deadly types of venom and will eat scorpions, including their stingers.

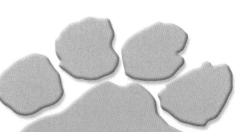

In 1995, a stampede of wild pigs killed 25-year-old Indonesian footballer Mistar at his team's training ground.

A possum 'plays dead' if it feels threatened. It lies completely still, hangs its tongue out, leaks dung and oozes green slime that smells of rotten flesh.

A female *echidna* (a hedgehog-sized mammal from Australia) grows a pouch on her stomach to keep the egg that she lays safe and sound. When the baby has grown and left, the pouch completely disappears.

Rats that hibernate together sometimes get their tails tied up in a big knot. If the rats urinate over themselves in the winter, they can freeze together in a block. Disgusting!

A chameleon can look in two directions at the same time, because its eyes can move separately.

When it is a tadpole, the Paradoxical frog of South America can grow to 25 centimetres/10 inches, but then shrinks to only 6 centimetres/2.5 inches when it becomes a fully grown frog!

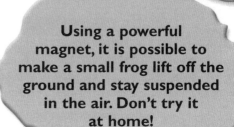

Using a powerful magnet, it is possible to make a small frog lift off the ground and stay suspended in the air. Don't try it at home!

If they are injured or damaged, newts can re-grow body parts, including legs, arms and even a new heart!

A rattlesnake's venom remains poisonous up to 25 years after it has died.

The *Polynesian skink* (a small lizard) has a bright blue tail which it can shed if it is attacked. The tail carries on wriggling after the lizard has gone, keeping the predator distracted.

Shaving a pregnant mouse makes her produce more milk and grow larger babies. It becomes a 'super mouse' because it can use more energy without overheating.

A porcupine can swallow 100 times the amount of poisonous hydrogen cyanide that is needed to kill a human – and suffer no ill effects.

Meat-eating animals won't eat an animal that has been struck by lightning.

A giraffe has special valves in its arteries so that its blood can be pumped up to its head. Without them, it would need a heart as big as its whole body!

The star-nosed mole has six times as many nerves going from its nose to its brain as a human has going from each hand to the brain.

The polar bear has the largest stomach capacity (in relation to its size) of any animal. It can kill and eat a large walrus or even a beluga whale.

Early explorers thought that a giraffe was a cross between a camel and a leopard and called it *cameleopard*!

The poisonous copperhead snake smells like freshly cut cucumber. Just don't put one in your salad!

When staff at the British Museum saw the first duck-billed platypus, they thought it was a fake animal and tried to pull off its bill!

Even though the armadillo eats mostly tiny termites and ants, it has more teeth than any other land mammal – around 100.

The *aye-aye* (a nocturnal mammal from Madagascar) has one very long, bony finger on one hand. It looks so scary that people used to believe they would die if they came into contact with one.

Tigers not only have striped fur, but also striped skin as well!

Being trampled by a cow is the cause of death for around 100 people each year.

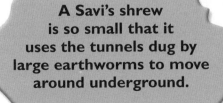

A Savi's shrew is so small that it uses the tunnels dug by large earthworms to move around underground.

A gecko always has its eyes closed! You won't notice, though, as its eyelids are clear. They help protect the gecko's eyes while allowing it to see.

Elephants are right- or left-tusked, just like people can be right- or left-handed!

Reindeer are one of the few animals that can eat moss. The moss contains chemicals that help to keep their body fluids warm.

A crocodile can't stick out its tongue.

Prairie dogs will only feed their young underground; if a baby tries to suckle above ground, the mother will slap it.

An alligator can go through 3,000 teeth in its lifetime. Maybe somebody should teach them to brush properly...

A zebra's stripes are unique – no two zebras look the same.

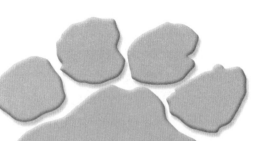

In winter, the croak of a golden tree frog sounds like a mallet chipping away at a rock, but in summer, it sounds like a tinkling bell!

A donkey can look at all four of its feet at once.

A kangaroo can't jump unless its tail is touching the ground.

Armadillos always give birth to quadruplets.

The sex of a crocodile's babies is determined by the temperature of a crocodile's nest, and how deeply the eggs are buried.

The rhinoceros belongs to the same animal family as the horse. Don't try putting a saddle on a rhino, though!

A mole can dig a 91-metre/ 300-foot-long tunnel in a single night.

Cows can walk up steps but not down steps.

Despite the myths, elephants are not afraid of mice...and do not have good memories!

The fastest reptile on the planet is the *spiny-tailed iguana* from Costa Rica, clocking in at a foot-burning 35 kilometre/ 22 miles per hour.

If you can get near the fur of a *binturong*, you'll smell popcorn. The Asian bearcat's smell comes from a gland near its tail.

A zebra's camouflage is effective because lions are colourblind. If a zebra stands completely still, a lion will see it as vertical blades of grass.

Horns never stop growing but antlers grow and are replaced every year.

An adult lion's roar is so loud that it can be heard up to 8 kilometres/ 5 miles away.

Elephants are the only mammals that can't jump.

All polar bears are left-handed.

In 1916, an elephant was tried and hanged for murder in Erwin, Tennessee, USA.

A hippo can drink up to 250 litres/66 gallons of water in a 24-hour period.

The underside of a horse's hoof is called a 'frog'!

In just 18 months, two rats can have over one million babies.

More people are killed every year by donkeys than in air crashes.

An elephant's tummy makes so much noise when it's digesting food that if there's any danger of a predator hearing it, it can immediately stop digesting. Ingenious! Try it yourself!

In relation to body size, tree shrews have the largest brain of any animal.

The Squirrel Day Festival is held every year in Olney, in Illinois, USA, to honour 200 resident albino squirrels. The festival even includes a blessing of the squirrels by a local priest.

The *sitatunga* (a species of antelope) can sleep underwater!

Rats can tread water for three days and swim for 0.8 kilometres/ half a mile without a rest.

It would take a year of milking 330 cows to gather the 2,499,322 litres/ 660,253 gallons of the white stuff you would need to fill an Olympic-sized swimming pool.

The *tarsier* (a small primate) has eyes so large that it is the equivalent of a human having eyes the size of grapefruits!

Elephants communicate at sound levels as low as 5hz. It's the noise made if you wave your hand up and down faster than five times a second. Even though you can't hear a noise, an elephant can!

Almost 50 per cent of all orang-utans have bone fractures due to regularly falling out of trees.

The tuatara lizard of New Zealand has two normal eyes and a third placed neatly on the top of its head!

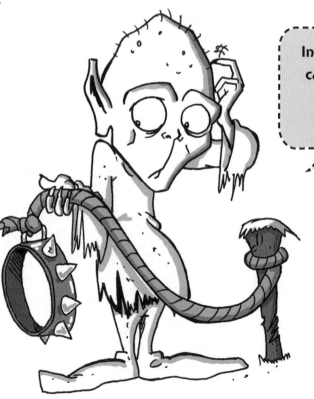

In May 1963, an American cow called Fawn was carried 0.8 kilometres/half a mile by a tornado and landed safely in a field. Five years later, another tornado carried her over a bus!

It takes a star-nosed mole just over a tenth of a second to identify, capture and eat its prey.

The word *hippopotamus* actually comes from two Greek words, meaning 'river horse'.

The only animal that can open Brazil nuts with its teeth is the large *agouti* rodent.

Hawaiian locals introduced mongooses to deal with their rat infestation. There was a slight problem: rats are *nocturnal* and hunt at night, while mongooses are *diurnal* and hunt during the day!

The *basenji*, a wild African dog, is the only species of dog that cannot bark.

A hippopotamus can eat up to 40 kilograms/88 pounds of short grass in one day. Who needs a lawnmower?

Because the golden mole lives in the desert and only comes out at night, its unused eyes are covered with skin and fur.

The Matamata turtle sucks in fish with a gulp so quick that it can't be seen with the human eye. Funnily, it swims so slowly that algae grows on its shell. What a weird creature!

The polar bear has only one predator – humans.

Pumas and leopards are the highest jumpers of the animal worlds – they can both reach a height of 5 metres/16.5 feet.

A grizzly bear can run as fast as a horse. Terrifying!

Arctic foxes do not hibernate – unlike many other Arctic animals, they can stand temperatures as low as –50 degrees Celsius/–58 degrees Fahrenheit.

Polar bears use their sense of smell to track down prey up to 30 kilometres/18 miles away. Even thick ice doesn't stop them from tracking their prey.

Lions cannot roar until they are two years old.

Because some species of millipede are poisonous, brown lemurs spit on them and roll them in their hands for a few minutes before eating them. Some scientists think it may be to combat the poison before eating, while others think the lemur rubs the poison on itself as a form of insect repellant.

The call of the male howler monkey can be heard up to 16 kilometres/10 miles away. That's twice as far as a lion's roar!

The collective name for a group of rhinoceros is a 'crash'.
Very appropriate!

Australia is home to a tiny marsupial called the *honey possum*. This sweet little creature lives entirely on pollen and nectar from flowers.

The *aye-aye* is the only primate that uses echolocation. This skill helps them find food buried up to 2 centimetres/0.3 inch inside trees.

When scared from their nest, common shrews will follow their mother in a line using their mouths to hold the tail of the family member in front.

The hyena is the only wild animal that cannot catch the disease *rabies*.

A scientist in Arizona, USA, has discovered that as well as making sounds to signal danger or friendship, prairie dogs also have calls that can identify the height and shirt colour of a passing human!

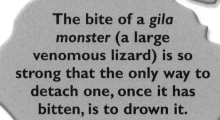

The bite of a *gila monster* (a large venomous lizard) is so strong that the only way to detach one, once it has bitten, is to drown it.

During the breeding season, *vixens* (female foxes) let out a long, eerie wail that sounds like a crying baby.

Not all hyenas are savages – the aardwolf hyena from southern Africa only eats tiny termites.

Even though they spend most of the year hiding them for winter, most squirrels can't remember where they hide half of their nuts.

A rare armadillo from Argentina is actually bright pink. The name of this odd little character? The *pink fairy armadillo*...

The gavial, a kind of crocodile from India, has over a hundred teeth.

When standing on its hind legs, a male kodiak bear is enormous – over 3 metres/10 feet tall. That's half a metre/2.5 feet taller than the world's tallest man!

When Feznik the movie star kangaroo was attacked by a wolf, he had plastic surgery to reconstruct his damaged lip.

Usually placid, leopard seals can sometimes attack without warning. In 2003, a biologist was killed after one snapped at her feet and dragged her under a sheet of ice.

Scientists used to think that pandas belonged to the raccoon family.

West African woolly bats are so small that they live in large spiderwebs.

Foxes and badgers have a scent gland which releases a liquid that glows fluorescent under ultraviolet light.

Black bears can swim for nearly 15 kilometres/ 9 miles without a rest. Think you're safe camping on an island? Think again…

Some shrews have red teeth because of the high concentration of iron in their bodies.

The minuscule *grasshopper mouse* defends its territory by howling like a tiny wolf.

Carpet vipers kill more people than any other type of snake does; their bite leads to uncontrollable bleeding.

If two chameleons get into a fight, they try to outperform each other by turning different colours. The defeated chameleon will turn pale grey before leaving the territory.

Elephants can smell water from as far away as 5 kilometres/3 miles.

More humans have been killed by foul-tempered hippos than they have by any other creature. Hippos like to overturn boats, trample people and even use their massive mouths to bite people's heads off.

A fully-grown male African elephant can weigh as much as 170 adult men.

Scientific tests have shown that one in 20 vervet monkeys will choose alcohol over any other drink, when given the choice. In one test, the monkeys drank so much that they passed out.

An anteater can eat 30,000 ants in one day.

Polar bears are the only mammals with hair on the soles of their feet.

A pig the size of a Shetland pony trapped a woman inside her rural Australian home in 2008. The animal had been overfed by neighbours and had become aggressive in its demand for food. When the owner of the house tried to leave her home the pig bit her leg and held her hostage in her home until the authorities came to her rescue!

Elephants are the only animals with four knees.

A fully grown moose was seen surfing down a river in 2006. The moose was spotted standing on a large chunk of ice, merrily making his way along the Namsen River in Norway.

Polar bears are practically undetectable by infrared cameras because of their transparent fur.

A fully grown python is able to swallow a large pig – whole.

A 545-kilogram/1,200-pound moose was found tangled in power lines 15 metres/50 feet in the air in Fairbanks, Alaska, in 2004. It is thought the moose got tangled in the lines and was hoisted into the air by the huge machine that was fixing the cables.

A polar bear's liver contains so much Vitamin A that it would be fatal if eaten by a human.

A giraffe's heart can pump 600 litres/160 gallons of blood in one minute.

The venom of the king cobra is so deadly that one gram of it can kill 150 people. Just to handle the substance with bare skin can put a person in a coma.

A bomb dropped by the Allies on Berlin during World War II killed every animal in the Berlin Zoo except the elephant, which escaped and roamed the city. Russian commanders ordered troops to protect it and shoot anyone who tried to harm the animal.

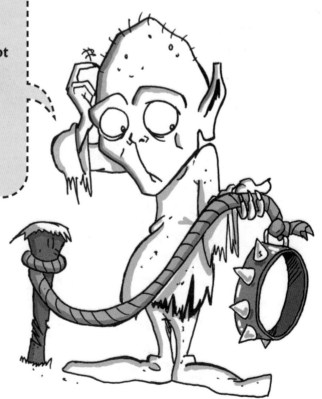

Atlantic white-sided dolphins like company so much that they have been spotted in groups of up to 1,000.

Koalas eat so much eucalyptus that if you stroke their fur your hands will smell sweet and minty.

A prairie dog settlement discovered in Texas, USA, in 1900 covered 64,750 sq kilometres/25,000 sq miles and had an estimated population of an astounding 400 million dogs!

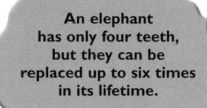

An elephant has only four teeth, but they can be replaced up to six times in its lifetime.

A rhino's horn is made of *keratin* – the same substance as your hair and nails.

The queen of a *naked mole rat* colony is the only one in the burrow to have babies. She keeps other females incapable of having babies using a special chemical in her urine.

Peculiar Pet
Facts

Dogs have been known to sense that their owner will suffer an epileptic seizure up to an hour before it actually happens.

Cat urine glows in the dark when ultraviolet light is shone on it.

Dogs in New York City produce 18 million kilograms/40 million pounds of poop every year. That's a lot of pooper-scoopers!

A rabbit's tongue contains 17,000 taste buds. That's 7,000 more than an average human!

Guinea pig meat is always on the menu in Peru and Bolivia, where the animals are bred as food.

Cats can make over 100 vocal sounds, while dogs can make only 10.

When two male dogs approach each other, the dog that wags its tail the slowest is the dominant one.

When early Australian settlers asked the native Aborigines the name of the colourful native birds, the Aborigines replied 'betchery-gah'. Only later did settlers discover that betchery-gah – which became *budgerigar* – actually meant 'good to eat'!

Customs officials at Melbourne airport were suspicious when they heard splashing sounds coming from a woman's skirt. It turned out she was smuggling 51 live tropical fish in a water-filled apron!

Rabbits love the taste of liquorice.

Hamsters can still recognize and remember their hamster relatives even if they have been separated for a long time.

Rudi the rabbit from Berlin in Germany is the world's largest pet rabbit, tipping the scales at a whopping 10 kilograms/22 pounds. Despite her 94-centimetre/3-foot-1-inch length, Rudi is still growing.

In 2006, Lewis the cat was put under house arrest by police in Connecticut, USA, because of his unprovoked attacks on local people. He was even placed in a line-up and picked out as the guilty party by a number of his victims.

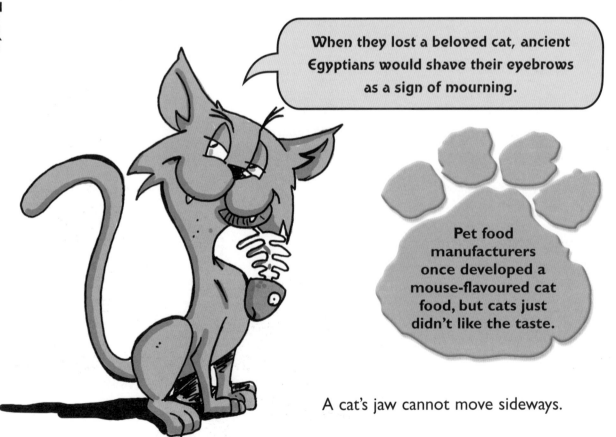

When they lost a beloved cat, ancient Egyptians would shave their eyebrows as a sign of mourning.

Pet food manufacturers once developed a mouse-flavoured cat food, but cats just didn't like the taste.

A cat's jaw cannot move sideways.

When hunting for the cause of a squeak in a tourist's car, Austrian mechanics soon discovered the driver's kitten trapped above one of the wheels. The kitten was shaken but had survived the car's 1,500-kilometre/900-mile long journey.

A cat's brain is actually more similar to a human brain than that of a dog. Cats and humans have identical regions in the brain responsible for emotion.

Every cat's noseprint is unique, just like a human fingerprint.

Statistics have shown that German shepherd dogs bite people more than any other breed of dog does. They are commonly kept as guard dogs…so maybe those who got bitten deserved it!

Cats are unable to survive on a purely meat-free diet.

Experiments have shown that dogs can locate the source of a sound in 6/100ths of a second, by using their ears like rotating radar dishes.

An average of 15 people die from dog bites every year in the USA.

Rabbits partially digest the grass they eat and then excrete it as soft, gluey pellets. They then eat these pellets to finish digesting their meal properly. Yummy!

The cat is the only domestic animal not mentioned in the Bible.

A cat is more likely to be injured if dropped from a small height than a great height. The extra height gives the cat time to realize what is going on and adjust its body to be able to land properly.

A Pekingese dog belonging to Henry Sleeper Harper and a Pomeranian dog belonging to Miss Margaret Hays are listed among the survivors of the *Titanic*.

It is against the law for a dog to fly a kite on most public beaches in the USA.

The *lhasa apso* dog was originally used by monks in Tibet to guard their temples.

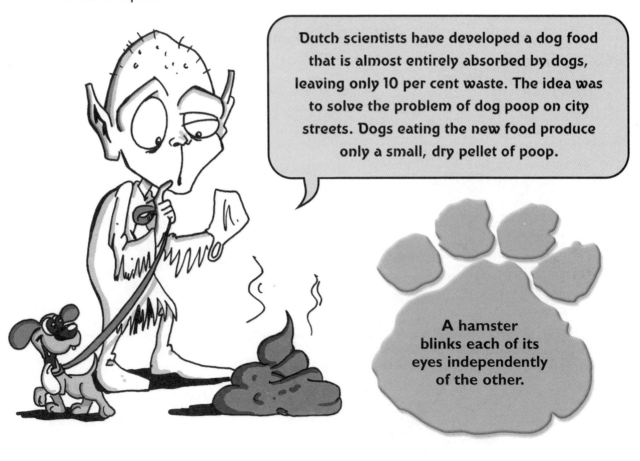

Dutch scientists have developed a dog food that is almost entirely absorbed by dogs, leaving only 10 per cent waste. The idea was to solve the problem of dog poop on city streets. Dogs eating the new food produce only a small, dry pellet of poop.

A hamster blinks each of its eyes independently of the other.

A cat's heart beats twice as fast as a human's.

Laikia the dog was the world's first ever astronaut. She was sent into space by the Russian government aboard a satellite in 1957.

Laikia was also the world's first space casualty, after dying from stress and overheating a few hours after take-off.

Cats have better memories than dogs. Tests have concluded that a dog's memory lasts no more than five minutes; a cat's can last as long as 16 hours.

The Canary Islands were not named after the canary bird, but after the large dogs that lived on the islands. In Latin, the name of the island group was *Canariae Insulae*, which translates as 'Island of Dogs'.

Chocolate can be deadly to a dog's heart and nervous system. Just a handful is enough to kill a small dog.

Contrary to popular belief, dogs do not sweat by panting – they sweat through the pads of their feet. Panting is used to lower their overall body temperature.

By the year 2002, dogs had killed more people in the USA than the great white shark has killed worldwide in the past 100 years.

In a single year, the average cat consumes nearly 28 times its own weight in food, and the same amount again in liquids.

Cats' whiskers can detect movements 2,000 times smaller than the width of a human hair.

A budgie by the name of Puck has the largest animal vocabulary, entering the Guinness Book of World Records in 1995 with a hefty 1,728 words.

Poshintang is a popular item on the menu in Korea. The soup is believed to cure summer heat ailments, improve male virility and women's complexions. The main ingredient in *poshintang*? Dog!

The bloodhound is the only animal whose evidence can be used in a US court.

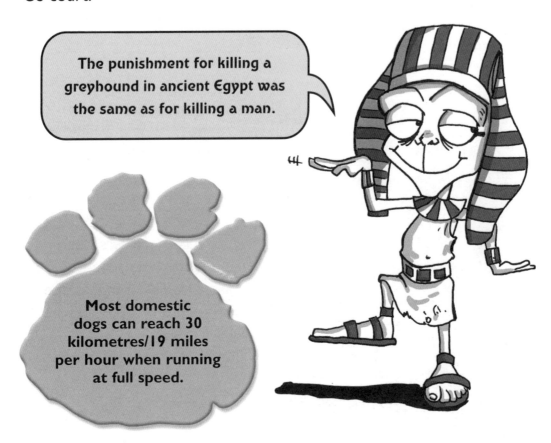

The punishment for killing a greyhound in ancient Egypt was the same as for killing a man.

Most domestic dogs can reach 30 kilometres/19 miles per hour when running at full speed.

A dog has up to 150 sq centimetres/23 sq inches of *olfactory membrane* – the area in the brain used to detect smells. A human has just 4 sq centimetres/0.62 sq inches.

Dalmatians were thought to be stupid dogs until it was discovered that they are genetically disposed to deafness.

A bakery near Frankfurt in Germany, offers treats such as tuna cakes and garlic cookies...just for dogs!

A cat's sense of smell is 14 times stronger than a human's.

An inventor in Sussex, England, designed a cat flap that was colour-sensitive. It would let his ginger cat in, but not his neighbour's black cat.

Siberian Huskies can live and work in temperatures as low as −60 degrees Celsius/−75 degrees Fahrenheit.

If a cat has differently coloured eyes, one of them will always be blue. The other can be green, orange or yellow.

A dog named Brutus became the world's highest-skydiving dog in 1997 after making a jump of 1,393 metres/4,572 feet.

The largest number of mice caught by a single cat is 28,899 over a 21-year period. That's about four mice a day, every day!

Domestic cats are the only species to hold their tails vertically while walking. Wild cats hold their tail horizontally, or tucked between their legs.

Kopi luwak coffee costs around £28/US$40 a cup and is made from the undigested coffee beans eaten by palm civet cats of Indonesia. Of course, you have to pick the beans from the cat's droppings before you can make a cup...

A cat would have to eat five mice to gain the same nutritional value as the average canned or dry cat food.

Although there are 100 different species of gerbil, the only one sold as a pet is a Mongolian variety called the *clawed jird*.

A goldfish can live for up to 40 years.

Cats do not like the smell of oranges and lemons.

Like humans, dogs and cats are either right- or left-handed.

Poodles were originally used in Europe as hunting dogs. Imagine!

Thirty-seven cats were employed to carry bundles of letters to villages in Liege, Belgium, in 1879. The cats proved pretty undisciplined and the service didn't last long. Yet the creators seemed surprised at the failure!

The first guide dog was presented to a blind person on 25 April 1938.

The longest-living rabbit on record was nearly 19 years old when he died.

The largest rabbit litter on record contained 24 babies. The average number of rabbits in a litter is about five!

Rabbits have over 150 different fur colour variations, but only five different eye colours.

Cats lose almost as much fluid through their saliva when they groom themselves as when they urinate.

Because of the position of their eyes, rabbits can see behind them without turning their heads.

If a cat is subjected to an electric current of 50 volts or more, its tail will point north. Do not try this at home!

Baby bunnies are totally odourless, which helps to protect them from predators.

In 2005, animal control officers investigated complaints of a foul smell coming from the house of 82-year-old Ruth Kneuven in Virginina, USA. Inside, they found nearly 500 cats, more than 100 of which were dead.

A rabbit thumps its hind legs to warn of danger.

A newborn ferret is so small that it can fit on to a teaspoon.

On average, a hamster will run up to 4.8 kilometres/3 miles a night on an exercise wheel.

During heavy downpours in 17th-century England, many of the stray cats and dogs would float down the narrow streets. This is where the expression 'raining cats and dogs' comes from.

Every dog's anal scent glands give off a unique smell. When a dog puts its tail between its legs, it does it to cover up its scent.

The proper name for a rabbit's fluffy tail is a 'scut'.

The USA is home to some very pampered pooches, with an estimated 1 million dogs having been named as the main beneficiary in their owners' wills!

The tallest living dog is Gibson, a harlequin Great Dane from California, USA. He measures 107 centimetres/ 3 feet, 6.2 inches tall!

Rabbits can alter their colour with the seasons to make it harder for predators to see them.

Rabbits have their own version of a purr – they will grind their teeth softly when petted.

Ferrets can sleep so deeply that they cannot be woken, even when picked up and jostled.

Cats are among the laziest animals, sleeping up to 18 hours a day.

A cat has a layer of extra cells in its eyes which absorb light, allowing it to see six times better at night time than a human.

Tortoiseshell cats are almost always female; only one in every 3,000 is male.

Three mice named Mia, Laska and Benji were sent into space by NASA in 1958.

Cats fall asleep quickly, but wake up frequently to check that their environment is safe from predators. That's where the term 'cat nap' comes from, meaning a short snooze.

A vet was hospitalized with hydrogen sulphide poisoning after entering a cottage that had 20 cats locked inside. The toxic fumes were from the cats' faeces.

Cats hate the noise made by crinkling aluminium foil.

Around 30 per cent of US pet owners admit to talking to their dogs or leaving messages on their answering machines for their dogs while they are away.

A group of rabbits is called a 'herd'.

Cats always clean themselves after they eat to remove any food odours that predators could smell and want to investigate!

Swiss vets have discovered that dogs suffer from stress. Living in a city and having a demanding owner are some of the reasons dogs suffer from headaches, stomach pain and other stress-related symptoms.

Based on an average life span of 11 years, the cost of owning a dog is £9,400/US$13,350.

Dogs have about 100 different facial expressions, most of them made using their ears. Unfortunately, bulldogs and pit bulls only have around ten.

A large number of pet ferrets are killed each year by reclining chairs. The ferret curls up under the chair and then gets squished when its unknowing owner puts the seat back.

Besides smelling with their noses, cats can smell with an additional organ called the *Jacobson's organ*, located in the upper part of their mouths.

Dachshund
means 'badger
dog' – the dogs were
originally bred for
digging badgers out
from their setts.

One human year is equal to 25 hamster years.

The world record for the highest jump made by a dog is 172 centimetres/5 feet, 8 inches. It was set by a holly grey at the Dog Challenge Finals in Florida, USA, in 2006.

A dog's sense of smell is one of the most advanced in the world. If a stew was cooking, a human would smell the overall aroma, whereas a dog would smell all of the ingredients individually.

Cats and dogs have been known to travel vast distances back to their original homes after their owners have moved house. No one knows how they do this so accurately.

Just like humans, guinea pigs can get scurvy if they do not get enough vitamin C in their diet.

The heaviest cat on record was Himmy, an Australian cat, who weighed 21.5 kilograms/47 pounds. No other cat has got so fat since!

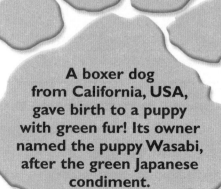

A horse in Coventry, England, had hay fever! The horse's owner had to give poor Teddy shredded newspaper to sleep on instead.

Two hundred cats were brought to the village of Sanjiang in China to solve the local rat problem. They were rewarded for their hard work with an enormous fish banquet!

A boxer dog from California, USA, gave birth to a puppy with green fur! Its owner named the puppy Wasabi, after the green Japanese condiment.

A group of ferrets is known as a 'business'.

A hunter from the village of Espelette in France was shot in the hip when one of his dogs stood on a loaded gun in the back of his car. Alarmingly, it is quite a common occurrence with hunters…

A cat laps up liquid using the underside of its tongue rather than the top.

Pet mice live for around two years, while their wild counterparts have an average life expectancy of just five months, due to the large number of predators in the wild.

The word *Spain* means 'land of hyraxes' (a type of small mammal). Early settlers were mistaken though – the small animals they were seeing weren't hyraxes but hares. So the name isn't right at all!

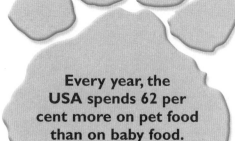

Every year, the USA spends 62 per cent more on pet food than on baby food.

In a pet insurance survey, more than 50 per cent of pet owners said they would rather be stranded on a desert island with their pet than with another person.

If a labrador and a poodle crossbreed, the result is called a labradoodle. True!

Tara the Labrador dog was injured when she tried to lick up biscuit crumbs that had fallen into a home paper shredder in Scotland in 2006.

In 1939, a student at Harvard University, USA, was dared to swallow a live goldfish for a bet. He did, and goldfish swallowing became a university craze.

In one day, a small rabbit will drink as much water as a dachsund dog.

Chipmunks take an average of 75 breaths a minute. A human takes just 8 to 14 breaths a minute.

Approximately 7 per cent of cats and 21 per cent of dogs snore.

An old town law in French Lick Springs, Indiana, USA, states that all black cats must wear bells on Friday the 13th.

When in unfamiliar territory, a hamster will rub its scent glands (found along its sides) against various objects. This leaves a scent trail the hamster can follow in order to come back the other way!

The word 'kitten' can actually mean a baby rabbit or beaver – not just a baby cat!

Weighing only 1.8 kilograms/ 4 pounds, the Singapura is the smallest breed of cat. That's the same as medium-sized pineapple.

The Saluki is the oldest breed of domestic dog, dating back to ancient Mesopotamia (around 3000BC). Before this, all dogs were actually wild wolves.

Following the goldfish-swallowing craze of the 1930s, a US State Senator presented a bill to protect goldfish from 'cruel and wanton consumption'.

The artificial rabbits used in greyhound races are sprayed with the scent of the anise plant to attract the dogs chasing them. They just love the smell!

When 13-year old cat Cadbury lost his miaow because of a rare throat condition, his owner Jean Kelly of Olney, England, paid for a series of operations to restore it. The cost? £10,000/US$17,000!

Ailurophobia is a fear of cats. Julius Caesar, Henry II, Charles XI, and Napoleon were all sufferers and would nearly faint in the presence of a cat.

The heaviest dog on record is an Old English Mastiff named Zorba, who weighed 155 kilograms/343 pounds. That's the same as two adult male humans.

There are over 40 million pet birds in the USA.

Cats love the smell of the plant *catmint* . It is often put in cats' toys!

The longest rabbit ears in the world belong to an English Lop called Nipper's Geronimo, from Bakersfield, California, USA. They measure 79 centimetres/31 inches long.

Baby hamsters are called 'puppies'.

The Latin name for a gerbil, *meriones unguiculatus*, means 'clawed warrior'.

In Pennsylvania, USA, dogs who want to meet in groups of three or more on private property must first have a permit signed by the mayor!

Catmint contains a chemical called called *trans-neptalactone*, the smell of which closely resembles a substance present in female cats' urine.

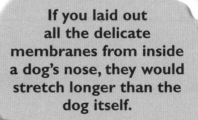

If you laid out all the delicate membranes from inside a dog's nose, they would stretch longer than the dog itself.

Cat owners from West Yorkshire couldn't bear to be parted from their beloved pussycat while on holiday abroad. Instead, they paid £37,000 for a new mobile home that would accommodate the pampered puss for a weeklong holiday.

When Ella Wendel from New York died in 1931 she left a sizeable fortune of US$23 million/£16.3 million to her beloved Toby – her pet poodle!

Sixty-six per cent of pet cats are female.

Recent research by a pet insurance company concluded that the most destructive pet dog is the Great Dane.

Walt Disney had a fear of mice.

Siamese cats are patterned according to their body heat! They are born white, then the coldest areas of their bodies turn a darker colour as they grow older. The hottest parts of their bodies stay white!

Cats are unable to taste sweet flavours.

A cat was sent through the mail in Germany when it sneaked into a package its owner was wrapping.

In the wild, a hamster's winter food store can grow to be huge. Some have been found to contain over to 1.5 million seeds!

Fifty-two per cent of pet owners in the USA admit that their pets get more exercise than they do.

Slimy, Stinky and Sick
Facts

The babies of the *boulengerula taitanus* (a worm-like amphibian) actually eat their own mother's skin. The babies use special teeth when born to squirm all over their mother's body and remove her flesh. Somehow the mother usually survives!

A frog juice market stall in Lima, in Peru, offers visitors a refreshing drink of skinned frogs blended into a smoothie. The locals claim this tasty treat cures a range of illnesses.

The world's largest ant colony was discovered in 2002. The interconnecting nests stretch 5,760 kilometres/3,579 miles from the Italian Riviera right through into northern Spain. The super-colony is home to several billion ants.

Roger Dier of Petaluna, California, USA, kept 1,300 rats. Not too bad until you realize he kept them all in his one-bedroom flat!

A duckbilled platypus can stuff its cheek pouches with 600 worms at once.

Every year 4.5 million litres/1 million gallons of dog urine goes into the parks of London.

Since the mid-1990s, many Tasmanian devils have died from *devil's facial tumour* disease. The mysterious illness causes large tumours to form around and inside the mouth, preventing feeding and causing the animals to die of starvation.

The *face fly* feeds on the mucus produced in a cow's eyes and nostrils.

In Tasmania, kangaroo manure has been used to make environmentally friendly paper.

The tongue louse is a type of parasite that crawls in through a fish's gills and then chews off the fish's tongue. It then spends the rest of its life acting as its victim's tongue while feeding off the blood supply of the fish.

Toxoplasma is a parasite that lives in rats' brains, changing their brains to make them less scared of cats. This means the rats are more likely to be caught and eaten, helping the parasite to move easily into cats' brains – their favourite place of all.

Japanese scientists have bred completely see-through frogs so that they can investigate their internal organs without having to kill and dissect them.

The African *zorilla* (a type of polecat) could be the smelliest creature on the planet. The stench secreted from its anal glands can be detected up to 1 kilometre/half a mile away.

The first recorded occurence of a frog being sick was when one was taken on a space flight.

A *scatologist* is a person who studies animal faeces.

Honeybees will surround any intruder in their colony and vibrate their bodies. The vibrations create so much heat that the invader is literally cooked to death.

A Hindu temple dedicated to the rat goddess Karni Mata in Deshnoke, India, houses more than 20,000 rats.

A *ribbon worm* (a sea creature) can eat 95 per cent of its own body – and still survive!

Cows produce 200 times more saliva than humans. Never ask a cow to blow out the candles on your birthday cake!

South African woman Elsie van Tonder had her nose bitten off by a seal in 2005 when she tried to help the stranded creature back into the water.

Porcupines looking for salt have been known to eat tool handles and clothes because of the salty human sweat on them.

In South Africa, termites are roasted and eaten as snacks, just like popcorn.

The *Argentinian wide-mouthed frog* will eat prey as large as itself, sometimes eating to the point of ripping open its stomach.

Skunks can accurately spray their smelly scent as far as 3 metres/10 feet.

Bracken Cave in Texas, USA, is home to 20 million bats. The floor is caked in a thick layer of bat faeces that the locals collect to use as fertilizer.

The Romans used crushed mouse brains as toothpaste.

The highly prized Malaysian liqueur *habu sake* is made from fermented viper venom.

A pinecone shortage in eastern Russia drove a gang of ravenous squirrels to attack and eat a stray dog.

Cow dung sets hard in hot countries and contains a natural mosquito repellent. Because of this, it is sometimes used to line floors and walls in buildings.

Birds do not urinate – their urine and faeces are all mixed together to make one sloppy dropping.

British artist Damien Hirst pickled a 4-metre/14-foot shark in formaldehyde. He called his work 'The Physical Impossibility of Death in the Mind of Someone Living'. The artwork was sold in 2004 for US$13 million/£9.2 million.

The African black rhinoceros excretes its own weight in dung every 48 hours. That's 682 kilograms/1,500 pounds a day!

The *female tahr* (a relative of the goat) from India lets the male know she is ready for mating by urinating on him. Nice!

The biggest tapeworm ever found inside a human body was 35 metres/115 feet long.

The giant cricket of Africa enjoys eating human hair. Nobody knows why!

In 2004, the polar bears in Singapore Zoo turned green! The change in colour was due to a type of algae growing in their hollow hair shafts.

If it cannot find enough food, a baby komodo dragon will eat its own brothers and sisters.

A baby naked mole rat has transparent skin – you can see right through it.

Four animals have blue tongues: the black bear, the chow chow dog, the giraffe and the blue-tongued skink.

Slugs produce two sorts of mucus: one is thin and watery and is used to move around, the other is thick and sticky and is used for protection.

British performance artist Paul Hurley wrapped himself in clingfilm and wriggled about in a soggy field nibbling soil for nine days in 2004. He called his performance 'Becoming Earthworm'.

Blister beetles secrete a poison that leaves a painful blister on the skin of its victim.

A vampire bat needs to eat every day or it will die. If it cannot find food it will flick the cheek of a well-fed bat to make it vomit. The hungry bat then happily munches on the sloppy seconds.

The *Peruvian booby bird* uses its own droppings to make its nest.

Chinese *geneticists* (scientists who study genes) have developed pigs that glow in the dark! The spooky porkers were created using injections of fluorescent green protein into pig embryos.

Some *stinkbugs* are able to spit their smelly goo as far as 30 centimetres/1 foot. Not bad for a bug often no more than 1.5 centimetres/half an inch long!

Whales vomit every 7 to 10 days to get rid of any indigestible items they may have swallowed.

Artist Chris Ofili from Manchester, England, is known for using elephant dung in many of his creations!

Three Peruvian shark fishermen who were lost at sea for 59 days in 2004 survived by eating turtle meat and drinking turtle blood.

Michael Fitzgerald of Evesham, in England, needed plastic surgery on his legs and arm after he was attacked by a badger in 2003. The badger attacked four more people in a 48-hour rampage before it was caught.

If you drink water with a leech in it, the tiny bloodsucker can attach to the inside of your mouth or throat and suck you dry from the inside.

A decomposing sperm whale exploded in Taiwan in 2004 as it was being transported for a post mortem. Nearby shops and cars were showered with blood, guts and blubber. A build-up of natural gases inside the whale was to blame.

Before synthetic bristles were invented, wild boar hair was used to make toothbrushes.

A *zoonosis* is any infectious disease that can be transferred between animals and people.

Locust swarms regularly cause traffic accidents in hot countries. There are so many of the flying insects around that cars often skid on the piles of squashed bugs that litter the highways.

To mark its territory, a hippopotamus spins its tail while pooping, as the spinning helps spread the stinky stuff around.

The fangs of the Australian funnel-web spider are so sharp that they have been known to penetrate human fingernails and soft shoes.

The pearl fish swims into a sea cucumber's anus and lives inside it during the daytime, coming out only at night. The sea cucumber breathes through its anus, so can't keep the fish out!

Cockroaches will eat each other when there's not much food around. After ripping open their victim's stomach they tear out their insides. Not very neighbourly!

The curly heaps of earth you find on the ground outside are called *worm casts*. They are actually little piles of worm poop.

Rats' urine often carries a serious and sometimes fatal infection called *Weil's disease*, which can cause jaundice and kidney damage.

A crocodile's digestive juices contain so much hydrochloric acid that they have been found to dissolve everything from iron spearheads to six-inch steel hooks.

Baby cockroaches feed on their parents' faeces to get the bacteria they need to help them digest plants and vegetables.

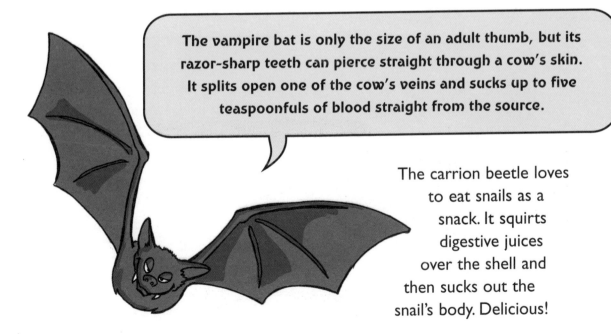

The vampire bat is only the size of an adult thumb, but its razor-sharp teeth can pierce straight through a cow's skin. It splits open one of the cow's veins and sucks up to five teaspoonfuls of blood straight from the source.

The carrion beetle loves to eat snails as a snack. It squirts digestive juices over the shell and then sucks out the snail's body. Delicious!

Dan Aeschleman from Illinois, USA, runs a business selling fox urine. Farmers and property owners buy the liquid to keep animals away, as they smell the urine and think a fox is near. He sells around 37,854 litres/10,000 gallons a year. Just don't ask how he collects it…

The venom of the brown recluse spiders is a *necrotic*, which means a bite will result in a large, open sore that will take months to heal and may require skin grafts.

Bee sting therapy can be used to treat medical conditions, such as multiple sclerosis and arthritis. Bee venom actually contains a substance called *melittin*, which reduces swelling. Bees are pressed on to the patient and allowed to sting away!

The New Zealand huhu beetle, otherwise known as the *haircutter*, has sharp hooks on its legs and antennae. If one lands in your hair, you'll need a haircut to get it out.

Mammal blood is red, lobster blood is blue, and insect blood is yellow.

In 2004, children at a nursery in Weston-super-Mare in England, were alarmed to see a three-headed, six-legged, mutant frog creeping out of their pond.

A vulture's stomach contains acids so strong that they can dissolve anything — even flesh containing the fatal *anthrax* disease. The disease can kill a human in just a few days after exposure.

Bored monkeys have been known to throw their faeces at anyone who happens to be passing...just for fun!

Cottonmouth snake venom is extremely effective at removing bloodstains from white clothes. Although getting the venom may cause more bloodstains, or worse...

Zombie worms live on the decaying bodies of dead whales. They bore deeply into the bones, then the microbes inside the worms help digest chemicals sucked out of the bones.

A pair of pigs in northern Italy became so enormous that they could not be moved and had to be taken from their sty in pieces. The pigs weighed 200 kilograms/ 440 pounds each.

A mummified dog was found inside a tree 6 metres/20 feet above the ground in Georgia, USA. The hollow tree was the perfect condition to keep the dog preserved for 20 years after its death.

A 12-month-old baby was saved at the Hadassah hospital in Jerusalem in 2004 after a snake attack. The boy survived because his nappy absorbed most of the venom.

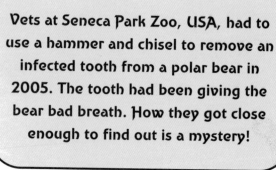

Vets at Seneca Park Zoo, USA, had to use a hammer and chisel to remove an infected tooth from a polar bear in 2005. The tooth had been giving the bear bad breath. How they got close enough to find out is a mystery!

Lightning struck a farm in northern Israel in 2004, causing the death of 10,000 chickens. Fried chicken anyone?

The head of a sperm whale contains up to 3 tons of a substance called *spermaceti*. It turns hard and waxy while the whale is diving in the cold depths and becomes oilier and more liquid as the whale gets warmer. The oil used to be an ingredient in some types of make-up.

Sailors on huge whaling ships used to cut the foreskins from male whales and use them as waterproof ponchos.

Cave swiftlets of Southeast Asia make nests from their own saliva. Locals use the dried nests to make the delicacy *bird's nest soup* – yes, it's a soup made from spit!

When a shark dies, it sinks so slowly to the bottom of the ocean that the salt water almost completely dissolves its corpse. The only parts that don't dissolve or get eaten are its teeth.

The *Coopers Nutmeg snail* lies hidden in the sand in shallow water until a ray passes by. It then attaches itself to the ray before making a small slash in its victim's skin and feeding on its blood.

Aborigines of Australia dig up the nests of honey ants then eat the tiny critters as a snack. The ants live on sweet foods like sugar and honey and apparently taste very sweet, if a little on the crunchy and wriggly side.

Fire ants are so called because a bite from one feels like a nasty burn on your skin.

Unlucky whales can be infected with *sinus flukes*. The fist-sized parasites like to live in the whale's airways, occasionally burrowing into their brains, too.

The *candiru* (an eel-like fish) lives in the Amazon River and is more feared than the pirahna. The transparent fish can smell urine in the water and heads straight for the source. It enters the body of its victim and burrows towards a major blood vessel to feed.

Romanian health officials were called to the apartment of 74-year-old Gyenge Lajos after he complained about a gas-like smell. The cause was soon discovered – a dead cow in the man's apartment that had been a gift from a friend. The carcass had started to rot, yet he was still cutting pieces from it to eat.

Fungus gnats from New Zealand dribble slime which collects in the roofs of the caves where they live. The gnats light up their bodies like glow-worms to attract insects, which get caught in the goo before being eaten.

The potato beetle larva protects itself from birds that want to eat it by covering itself in its own poisonous faeces.

An elephant can produce a 38-kilogram/83-pound pile of poop in one go.

If a predator gets too close to a vulture, it will protect itself by trying to vomit in the predator's eyes, causing a burning sensation.

The hairy-handed crab has hairy pads on its pincers, where tiny bits of food collect. When food is scarce, the crab nibbles on the leftovers.

Mosquitoes love stinky human feet because of the enzymes found on them.

According to an old Californian law, it is illegal to pile horse manure more than 1.82 metres/6 feet high on any street corner.

The *mabra elephantophila moth* drinks the tears of elephants. In order to get vital salts, the moth actually makes the elephant cry by dragging its *proboscis* (needle-like snout) across the elephant's eyeball.

A German shepherd dog was successfully trained to sniff out sheep droppings that were infected with worms on an Australian sheep farm. Useful, but still gross…

The fart of a female southern pine beetle contains a pheromone called *frontalin*, which attracts male beetles.

Dracula ants, discovered in Madagascar in 1993, punch holes in their own larvae and feed off their blood.

Vampire bats urinate the whole time that they're sucking blood. This ensures they don't get so full of blood that they're too heavy to fly.

In 2005, Atascaderos in Mexico was plagued by rats that had learnt to avoid poison. It was estimated that at one point there were 500,000 rats roaming the village.

Scientists have created genetically engineered mice whose hearts flash green each time they beat. Sounds like they'd be great fun at parties!

When a toad is sick, it vomits up its entire stomach. It hangs out of its mouth for a short time before being swallowed back down.

Flies eat by vomiting on their food. The chemicals in their vomit start to dissolve whatever is in front of them. When it's sloppy, they suck it all up again. That's why it's a really bad idea to eat anything a fly has been sitting on!

In 1954, Russian scientist Vladimir Demikhov created a two-headed dog by grafting the head and front legs of a puppy onto a fully grown dog. The animal lived for six days, but later he created one that lived for a month. Freaky!

Baboons have rough, nerveless *callouses* (thick skin) on their bottoms so that they can sit anywhere in total comfort!

A pond in Hamburg was dubbed 'the pond of death' in 2004 when hundreds of its toads exploded after being attacked by crows. The unlucky crows scattered toad guts more than 3 metres/10 feet away.

A jellyfish excretes faeces through its mouth! It has only one opening and uses it for all its bodily functions.

Light-coloured spots on surfaces of food show a fly has vomited on it; dark-coloured spots are fly faeces. Yummy!

Animal manure produces heat as it decomposes. Sometimes large piles of manure burst into flames when the heat reacts with the naturally occurring methane gas.

The yellow-bellied toad wards off predators by producing a nasty garlic-smelling foam.

The female *Surinam toad* fixes her eggs on her back, where the spongy flesh swells, and absorbs them. When the froglets hatch, they leave behind holes in their mother that they use as shelter until they are large enough to fend for themselves.

In 2006, a Kenyan elephant slipped into a septic tank (a sewage container) while trying to steal bananas on a farm. The unlucky elephant was then killed and eaten by villagers. Nicely marinated, no doubt!

Soldier flies like to lay their eggs in human faeces. The larvae are often found in bathrooms as they crawl up the sewage pipes.

Around four times a year, adult toads will shed their skin then eat it.

Scientists sometimes pick apart owl pellets (undigested food that owls vomit) to find out what they've been feeding on. You can even buy owl pellets to examine at home. Yuck!

While sleeping, humans swallow an average of 14 bugs per year.

A woman found a lunch box in an Edinburgh street in 2006 – and opened it to find it was full of baby boa constrictors. Snake sandwich, anyone?

A woman tried on a pair of jeans in a shop in Okinawa, Japan, only to be stung in the leg by a scorpion that was hiding inside them! Although the sting was not fatal, the woman was hospitalized for several days.

Cows release 50 million tonnes of methane gas every year.

Maggots of the screw-worm fly eat healthy flesh. If they infest an animal or human wound, they burrow in and destroy the healthy tissue around it, making the wound far worse.

A strange-smelling suitcase abandoned at Amsterdam's Schipol airport in 2003 was found to contain 2,000 baboons' noses. It's believed the animal parts, en route from Nigeria to the United States, would have been used in traditional medicines.

Green muscardine disease is a fungus that kills insects. The spores enter the insect and grow inside it, eventually covering the insect's outer body with green mould and completely suffocating it.

Authorities in Iowa, USA, investigated complaints by neighbours only to discover that a house contained 350 snakes and 500 rodents. Bizarrely, only six illegal snakes were removed, as all the animals were well looked after.

Cow parts caused traffic chaos when a meat lorry crashed near San Francisco and scattered its cargo across the freeway.

One of the favourite dishes of Japanese Emperor Hirohito was rice cooked with wasps. Spicy!

Planarian worms shoot a tube out of their throats which holds down their prey. Then they drip enzymes all over their victim to soften it up before tearing chunks off it to eat.

Fried spiders are regularly eaten as a delicacy in Cambodia. Apparently they taste like nuts.

Bluebottle and greenbottle flies, who are common visitors to our homes, bring with them the bacteria and yuckiness from the rotting meat, carcasses and animal faeces where they lay their eggs.

In the UK alone, domestic cats kill 57 million mammals a year, 27 million birds and 5 million reptiles and amphibians.

In a US survey, at least 63 per cent of dog owners admitted to kissing their dogs. When asked to state where they kissed them, 29 per cent listed the place 'other'! Eeewww!

Scientist Robert Cornish carried out an experiment in the 1930s at the University of California to try to bring animals back from the dead by moving their bodies up and down on a seesaw. As you can probably guess, it didn't quite work...

It is impossible to filter all traces of fish *dander* (flaking scales) from our drinking water. Pass the dandruff shampoo...

It has been discovered that herring fart frequently, but only at night.

Dogs like eating cat poop because it's high in protein.

C. Manoharan of India set a new world record in 2003 by swallowing 200 live earthworms in just over 20 seconds.

Sharks don't have a urinary tract, so they have to urinate straight through their skin.

Jackals will eat decomposing or diseased flesh even if it has been rotting for days. They pass this practice along to their pups by feeding their young with their own vomit every few hours to prevent starvation. If the pups get full, no worries – the jackals will just eat their regurgitation.

Because maggots have no teeth, they ooze *ferment* (saliva) from their mouths to liquidize their food before sucking it up.

The horned lizard from South America can shoot blood out of its eyes when under attack.

An elephant produces around 150 kilograms/330 pounds of dung every day.

A mosquito can drink one and a half times its own weight in blood in a single meal.

A hyena can chew a broken bottle without hurting itself.

Female Egyptian vultures are attracted to the male with the yellowest face. Unfortunately for the males they have to eat their own poo to achieve this look!

Giraffes have such long and flexible tongues that they can lick inside their own ears. Nobody knows what they taste like though.

Armadillos produce so much saliva that they have a small pocket at the back of their tongue to store it in.

Chinese scientists have found that common houseflies carry a minimum of 1,941,000 different bacteria on their bodies.

Cows only partly digest the grass they eat – after swallowing, they vomit it back up into their mouths, chew it, then swallow it all over again.